ONE POT WONDERS

ONE POT WONDERS

100 comforting recipes to curl up with

LINDSEY BAREHAM

Photography by Chris Terry

MICHAEL JOSEPH
an imprint of
PENGUIN BOOKS

For my sister Sally

MICHAEL JOSEPH

Published by the Penguin Group

Penguin Books Ltd, 80 Strand, London WC2R 0RL, England

Penguin Group (USA) Inc., 375 Hudson Street, New York, New York 10014, USA

Penguin Group (Canada), 90 Eglinton Avenue East, Suite 700, Toronto, Ontario, Canada M4P 2YR
(a division of Pearson Penguin Canada Inc.)

Penguin Ireland, 25 St Stephen's Green, Dublin 2, Ireland (a division of Penguin Books Ltd)

Penguin Group (Australia), 707 Collins Street, Melbourne, Victoria 3008, Australia
(a division of Pearson Australia Group Pty Ltd)

Penguin Books India Pvt Ltd, 11 Community Centre,
Panchsheel Park, New Delhi –110 017, India

Penguin Group (NZ), 67 Apollo Drive, Rosedale, Auckland 0632, New Zealand
(a division of Pearson New Zealand Ltd)

Penguin Books (South Africa) (Pty) Ltd, Block D, Rosebank Office Park, 181 Jan Smuts Avenue,
Parktown North, Gauteng 2193, South Africa

Penguin Books Ltd, Registered Offices: 80 Strand, London WC2R 0RL, England

www.penguin.com

First published 2014

001

Copyright © Lindsey Bareham, 2014
Photography © Chris Terry, 2014
The moral right of the author has been asserted

Set in MrsEaves and Kailey
Colour reproduction by Altaimage Ltd
Printed in Italy by Printer Trento Srl

A CIP catalogue record for this book is available from the British Library

ISBN: 978–0–718–17890–1

Penguin Books is committed to a sustainable future
for our business, our readers and our planet. This
book is made from Forest Stewardship Council™
certified paper.

Contents

Introduction

It was the camping holidays of my childhood and my mother's propensity for cooking everything in a pressure cooker that probably instilled in me a passion for one pot cooking. My sons were brought up on big chunky soups and grew to love stews, particularly when I called them by another name, like tagine or *cocido*, making supper sound exotic as if we were eating in a restaurant. They loved to come home from school to the smell of a richly aromatic stew simmering away on the back burner. It is still my favourite way of cooking and eating. After all, what's not to love about slow-cooked food that is easy to eat with a fork and spoon or scooped up with crusty bread?

One pot cooking can be as simple or as complicated as you like and can involve all styles of cooking, from casserole-all-sorts, to gratins and roasts, steamed dishes, pizza, *paella* and stir-frys. Even salads can be classified as one pot wonders.

I once spent three months cooking with a plug-in two-burner hotplate that moved around the house with me when I had extensive work done on my kitchen-dining room. Since then, I have become a stickler for adapting my recipes to work in one pot. Not only is it a simple way of saving fuel but it also cuts down on the worst kind of washing-up. Once you get a taste for one pot cooking, and you will, it might change your entire cookery outlook. I'd recommend taking a long, hard look at your pots and pans. My current favourite, apart from my beloved Le Creuset casseroles, is a huge, heavy-bottomed, oven-proof frying pan with a glass lid. I use it for everything from risotto to goulash.

The book begins with a wide-ranging interpretation of **FRY-UPS**, ringing the changes with some surprising combinations, like salami and mushroom hash, quickly fried smoked mackerel croquettes with beetroot purée, and slurpy dishes like Moorish meatballs with peas.

On a healthier note, I love making a meal of **SALADS**, with elaborate combinations like ginger prawns with Vietnamese noodles, watercress tabbouleh with chicken kebabs and Szechuan chicken salad with peanut and sesame.

BAKES, like stews, are possibly the simplest style of one pot cooking, when all the ingredients go into a pot at the same time. They don't have to take an age to cook. Some, like baked Provençal sea bass with potatoes; slipper aubergine, tomato and goat's cheese, and roast meatballs with sweet potatoes and lemon couscous, are on the table in almost the same time that it takes to heat up a ready meal. There are some surprises in this section of the book. Dishes like pulled belly pork sliders with apple sauce rub along with old-fashioned comfort dishes like Lancashire hotpot, steak and mushroom cobbler pie and a stupendous cumin slow-roasted shoulder of lamb with couscous to drink up the luscious juices.

BIG SOUPS are possibly my favourite way of cooking. It's a great way of eating economically while keeping in touch with the seasons. I like building layers of flavour with spices and fresh herbs, combinations like green minestrone with watercress pesto, beetroot soup with cumin lamb meatballs, Japanese fish broth with barley, and pork, chorizo and peas.

STEWS are the mainstay of one pot cooking and my selection draws inspiration from all around the world: Armenian chicken and aubergine stew, Korean chicken with pear sauce, pork stifado from Greece, a great veal *spezzatino* from Italy and traditional British beef stew with parsley, carrots and thyme dumplings.

CURRIES are basically spicy stews and the selection ranges from classy vegetarian dishes like coconut egg masala and aubergine curry, to Mumbai prawn pasta, Sri Lankan chicken curry with sweet potato and spinach and Thai duck curry with cucumber relish. The finale is a knock-out aromatic Hindu lamb curry with tomatoes.

While all the recipes in this book can be cooked in one pot or pan, it is sometimes used twice. A bit of deft pot-juggling is required to meet the one pot restriction for some **PASTA** dishes. Many, though, like crab with conchiglie and artichoke linguine with green olives, don't have a cooked sauce, so only the pasta needs a pan. Others, like black pasta with garlic olive oil and chilli, require the pasta to be cooked first and kept warm while the sauce is quickly made in the same pan. Some, like duck *ragu*, which combine pasta and sauce, use the same pan twice; first to cook the sauce and again to cook the pasta, then the two combined to finish the dish.

Very few pasta dishes work like risotto, when all the ingredients cook together. The most dramatic is *fideua* from Valencia, the home of *paella*. And that is what it is; *paella* made with pasta instead of rice.

It's easy, though, to cheat with sachets of cooked pasta and increasingly, of various types of NOODLES. They come ready for the wok or a quick soak in hot water before they're ready to eat. Some are wheat based, others are snowy-white rice noodles, the type that predominate in Thai cooking and look so unpromising in their pre-cooked, dry state. It's useful to have a few packs of the ambient, ready soaked, no-cook noodles in the food cupboard for quick slurpy noodle suppers like salmon confit, brown shrimp and samphire noodles, or intriguingly flavoured pomegranate and ginger lamb noodles.

Apart from convenience pasta and noodles, I'm very keen on stashing other ways of providing essential no-cook bulk to go with stews and curries. I recommend keeping a packet or two of couscous and bulgur wheat in the store cupboard. Both only require a soak in boiling water or stock before they are ready to eat hot, warm or cold. I'm also a big fan of ready-cooked lentils (sold in ambient pouches); even rice can be bought ready cooked. The RICE section of the book is one of my favourites, with dishes as diverse as Louisiana jambalaya, *paella bianco*, risotto with sausage, beans and red wine, a lovely summer kedgeree with lime, and a Moroccan-flavoured chicken pilaff.

It was incredibly difficult to make the final selection of recipes to include in *One Pot Wonders*, and the PUDDING section was hardest of all. I wanted a good cross-section but many puddings are chosen for their classy looks. The selection begins with a pretty fruit salad of lychees, melon and stem ginger and includes a fabulous rhubarb trifle with a lemon syllabub topping, a dramatic Black Swan pavlova, comforting Malva pudding from South Africa, and a stunning pear and ginger cheesecake.

And finally, a useful tip for warming a serving bowl or platter is to give it a quick soak in hot water, and the easiest way to keep sauce or pasta warm, should you need to, is in a hot bowl with a stretch of clingfilm to keep the warmth in.

Lindsey Bareham, September 2013

Fry-ups

DEVIL'S NEST

AUBERGINE *KUKU* WITH
POMEGRANATE AND FETA

SMOKED MACKEREL CROQUETTES
WITH BEETROOT PURÉE

FLAT PEAS AND SOLE,
LIME AND GINGER STIR-FRY

POACHED SAUSAGES, CELERY
AND POTATOES

CHICKEN AND CHORIZO BULGUR
WITH BROAD BEANS

SALAMI AND MUSHROOM HASH

MOORISH MEATBALLS WITH
MINTED PEAS

I once read an interview with Jon Hamm, the actor who plays the suave, hard-drinking, chain-smoking Don Draper in *Mad Men*, the brilliant depiction of a cutting-edge advertising agency in fifties and sixties Manhattan. The interview had taken place at a café in Silver Lake, a boho-chic part of Los Angeles. Hamm ordered Devil's Nest, described as a scramble of avocado, sour cream and spicy sausage, which inspired this perfect home-alone very nearly store-cupboard one-pan dish.

My portion control is very generous, in fact there is enough for two unless you are exceptionally hungry or greedy (I am often both). I make it with chorizo, coriander, a dribble of sweet chilli dipping sauce and dollop of sour cream to complement the almost-guacamole and scrambled eggs. To make this for more, just double up all the ingredients in proportion.

DEVIL'S NEST SERVES 2

PREP: 15 MINUTES
COOK: 10 MINUTES

• *100g sliced chorizo*
• *2 small ripe avocado*
• *1 lime*
• *8 cherry tomatoes*
• *a few sprigs of coriander*
• *4–6 large eggs*
• *salt and freshly ground black pepper*
• *a large knob of butter*
• *2 large slices of sourdough toast*
• *1 clove of garlic*
• *1 tablespoon olive oil*
• *a dribble of sweet chilli sauce*
• *2 tablespoons soured cream or crème fraîche*

Heat a medium-sized saucepan while you quarter the chorizo slices. Scatter them into the hot pan – no need for oil – tossing for about 30 seconds until crisp. Tip onto kitchen paper to drain. Run a knife round the avocado, twist it apart, remove the stone and chop the flesh in the skin, lightly crushing some of the cubes as you scrape it into a bowl. Season generously with lime.

Quarter the cherry tomatoes, chop the coriander leaves and stir both into the avocado. Whisk the eggs and season with salt and freshly ground black pepper. Melt the butter in the pan and scramble the eggs in the usual way. Stir in the chorizo. Toast the bread, then rub one side with garlic and dribble with olive oil. Spoon the eggs into the middle of two plates, top with the avocado mixture and dribble with sweet chilli sauce. Scatter over the coriander and top with the soured cream or crème fraîche. Serve the bruschetta on the side.

Kuku is the Persian name for a deep stuffed omelette that is light on egg and thick with filling. It's a bit like a Spanish tortilla (potato and onion omelette) but *kuku* is easier to get right. This one is made with aubergine, spring onions, feta and spinach, with a colourful garnish of pomegranate seeds, mint and a final crumble of feta. It is good eaten hot, warm or cold. In fact, it's perfect picnic food because it's sturdy enough to transport without spoiling: add the garnish at the last minute.

AUBERGINE *KUKU* WITH POMEGRANATE AND FETA SERVES 4–6

PREP: 30 MINUTES
COOK: 35 MINUTES

• 2 aubergines (500g)
• salt and freshly ground black pepper
• 125g bunch of spring onions
• 3 tablespoons olive oil
• 6 eggs
• 150g Greek feta cheese
• 50g pomegranate seeds
• a few mint leaves

Chop the aubergines into small kebab-size chunks. Half fill a large bowl with water, stir in a tablespoon of salt and the aubergine. Keep immersed with a plate and leave for at least 20 minutes; this helps draw liquid out of the aubergine so it absorbs less oil as it fries. Drain thoroughly, rinse and pat dry with kitchen paper.

Trim and finely slice the spring onions. Soften them in a tablespoon of the olive oil in a heavy-bottomed frying pan, adding a pinch of salt. Tip the onions onto a plate to cool. Whisk the eggs in a mixing bowl. Crumble 100g of feta over the top and season with salt and freshly ground black pepper.

Swirl another tablespoon of the oil around the pan and add the aubergine. Increase the heat slightly and cook, tossing constantly to begin with and regularly as the pieces soften and shrink. Adjust the heat so the aubergine cooks evenly, continuing until soft, dark and juicy. Tip the spring onions into the egg mixture, then the aubergines and stir them together.

Swirl the final tablespoon of oil around the pan and pour in the egg mixture. Shake to settle it, and cook for 3 to 4 minutes over a medium-low heat until the *kuku* is beginning to set around the edge. Complete the cooking under a preheated grill, allowing a maximum 5 minutes, until the egg is just set. Let it rest for a couple of minutes, then slide a metal spatula around and under the omelette to loosen it.

Place a lid that fits inside the pan over the top, quickly invert the pan, then slide the omelette the right way up onto a plate. Scatter pomegranate seeds, the remaining crumbled feta and chopped mint over the top. Serve in wedges.

These crusty little croquettes ooze a soft and creamy filling when you bite into them, like ice cream between wafers. Smoked mackerel's strong flavour is subdued by the mashed potato but interestingly offset by creamed horseradish. I like to serve the croquettes piled on a platter with lemon wedges to squeeze over the top and a mound of fluffy puréed beetroot. The quantities given make 8 normal-size fishcakes.

SMOKED MACKEREL CROQUETTES WITH BEETROOT PURÉE SERVES 4

PREP: 25 MINUTES, PLUS
30 MINUTES TO CHILL
COOK: 25 MINUTES

- *500g King Edward potatoes*
- *salt and freshly ground black pepper*
- *15g butter*
- *2 tablespoons milk*
- *½ lemon*
- *340g smoked mackerel fillets*
- *1 egg*
- *2 tablespoons creamed horseradish*
- *flour for dusting*
- *100g fine breadcrumbs*
- *oil for frying*
- *lemon wedges to serve*

for the beetroot purée:
- *400g boiled beetroot*
- *2 tablespoons creamed horseradish*
- *1 lemon*
- *a splash of Tabasco*

Peel the potatoes and cut them into even-size pieces. Rinse, then boil them in salted water in a spacious, lidded frying or sauté pan until they are just tender, before they get waterlogged and fall apart. Melt the butter with the milk. Drain the potatoes and leave for 5 minutes before mashing them with the butter and milk mixture. Beat in the juice from the half-lemon, then spread the mash in a mixing bowl to cool slightly.

Flake the fish off its skin over the top, watching out for bones. Separate the egg: put the white into a mixing bowl, the yolk with the fish. Add the creamed horseradish, plenty of freshly ground black pepper, and fold together, then mix vigorously so the fish breaks down further against the warm mash.

Form the mixture into a ball. Dust a work surface lavishly with flour. Halve the mixture and, with floured hands, roll and pat both pieces into a thick sausage. Cut each piece into 4. Divide each into 3, patting and rounding to make 24 plump little mini-fishcakes (croquettes). (Alternatively, pat it into 8 normal-size fishcakes.) Chill for at least 15 minutes.

Whisk the egg white until foamy. Spread the breadcrumbs on a plate. Pass the croquettes through the egg, then press them into the crumbs. Shallow-fry them in batches in hot oil until they are golden all over. Pile them onto a warmed serving platter with lemon wedges and the beetroot purée.

To make the purée, coarsely chop the beetroot and pile it into the bowl of a food processor. Add the creamed horseradish, 1½ tablespoons of lemon juice, a tablespoon of hot water, a splash of Tabasco and a generous seasoning of salt. Blitz for several minutes to purée. Taste and adjust the seasoning with more lemon, salt and Tabasco.

Fry-ups

Flat peas, or mangetout, as most people call them, are perfect in stir-fries, staying crisp and crunchy, lending their sweet pea flavour. I don't buy them often, preferring to stay with seasonal British vegetables, but weakened as I pictured them in my wok with shiny white sole fillets and scraps of ginger, underpinned by the nutty flavour of toasted sesame oil and mirin, a sweet yet tangy Japanese rice wine.

As with all stir-fries, it's essential to do all the chopping and slicing before you start cooking. Once everything hits the pan, the food is ready in minutes. For a light, healthy supper, serve it as it is; for a more robust meal, it goes well with boiled basmati rice or super-quick rice noodles.

FLAT PEAS AND SOLE, LIME AND GINGER STIR-FRY SERVES 2

PREP: 15 MINUTES
COOK: 10 MINUTES

• 2 medium mushrooms
• 4 spring onions
• 2 cloves of garlic
• 20g ginger
• 150g flat peas (mangetout)
• 250g sole fillets
• 1 tablespoon toasted sesame oil
• 2 tablespoons mirin
• 2 tablespoons lime juice
• 1 tablespoon vegetable oil
• soy sauce, to serve

Wipe the mushrooms and slice them chunkily into 4 or 5 pieces. Trim and finely slice the spring onions, including the green part. Crack the garlic, flake away the skin, and finely chop it. Peel the ginger and slice it into paper-thin scraps. Top and tail the flat peas, removing stringy edges, then halve lengthways on the diagonal. Following the natural lines of the fish fillets, slice them into double-bite-size pieces. Mix the sesame oil, mirin and lime juice together.

Heat the wok over a medium-high heat. Add the vegetable oil and swirl it around the pan, then tip in the mushrooms, spring onions, garlic and ginger. Toss constantly, adjusting the heat so the food cooks without burning. After a couple of minutes, when the mushrooms darken and look juicy and the spring onions are beginning to soften, add the peas. Continue tossing, then add the fish and mirin mixture. Keep scooping and tossing, and after a couple of minutes, when the fish has firmed and the pieces are just cooked through, the dish is ready. Scoop everything out of the pan into bowls. Pass round the soy sauce.

It is not worth making this unless you take the trouble to buy meaty pork sausages made with proper casings that won't ooze fat and spoil the fresh flavours of this modest but surprisingly delicious combination. You begin by caramelizing finely sliced onion with chunks of sausage. Then you poach big pieces of celery and diced potato with them. The celery gives the food a fresh vitality that keeps the dish light and elegant, while a garnish of chives and sage injects a final burst of interest. To make this for more people, just scale up the ingredients in proportion.

POACHED SAUSAGES, CELERY AND POTATOES SERVES 2

PREP: 20 MINUTES
COOK: 30 MINUTES

- 2 onions (200g)
- 1 tablespoon olive oil
- 8 Gloucester Old Spot pork sausages
- 4 stalks of celery
- 4 large Charlotte potatoes (350g)
- salt
- 1 tablespoon snipped chives
- a few small sage leaves

Peel, halve and finely slice the onions. Heat the oil in a spacious lidded sauté pan over a medium heat and stir in the onions. Cook, stirring often, while you cut the links between the sausages and twist each one into 4 small plump pieces. Don't worry if the ends burst. Peel the celery with a potato peeler and cut it on the diagonal into pieces about 8cm long. Peel the potatoes. Rinse, then cut them into kebab-sized chunks.

Stir the sausages into the wilting onions, increasing the heat slightly so that they firm up quickly and begin to colour. Add the celery and cook for a few minutes to draw out the juices. Put in the potatoes and just cover them with water. Season with salt. Establish a gentle simmer, cover the pan and cook for 15 to 20 minutes until the potatoes are tender and the sausages cooked through.

Chop the sage leaves. Taste the pan juices and add more salt if necessary. Simmer uncovered for a few minutes, then scatter with the chives and the chopped sage leaves.

Pilaff-meets-risotto describes this intriguing dish. It's a great way of making a modest amount of chicken go a long way with a mix of store-cupboard ingredients you might not have thought to combine. I keep chorizo in the fridge on standby to give a flavour boost to dishes like this. Its spicy, oily juices go well with the nutty taste of bulgur cracked wheat. Quickly peeled broad beans add creaminess while looking bright and summery against everything else. The making of the dish, though, is Moroccan-style salt-preserved lemon. Its salty, tangy, lemony flavour pings the taste-buds into life. The final ingredient is dramatic black garlic. I love its dense, almost chewy texture and mellow garlic flavour. It's available from Tesco, Waitrose and Ocado, or from www.blackgarlic.co.uk, but the dish will still be good without it.

CHICKEN AND CHORIZO BULGUR
WITH BROAD BEANS SERVES 4

PREP: 20 MINUTES
COOK: 40 MINUTES

- salt
- 300g podded fresh or frozen broad beans
- 200g Iberico chorizo
- 2 onions (150g)
- 1 tablespoon olive oil
- 600g chicken thigh fillet
- 3 Moroccan-style salt-preserved lemons
- 8 cloves of black garlic or 2 cloves of garlic
- 500ml chicken stock
- 250g bulgur wheat
- 50g flat-leaf parsley

Boil a full kettle and three-quarters fill a spacious sauté pan with boiling water. Add a teaspoon of salt and the beans. Scoop them onto a plate as they rise to the surface; this takes seconds with frozen beans and a couple of minutes with fresh. Leave them to cool.

Run a knife down the chorizo and peel off the skin. Slice it thickly, then halve the slices. Peel, halve and thinly slice the onions. Heat the oil in the empty sauté pan over a medium heat and add the onion. Cook, stirring a couple of times, for 8 minutes until it is wilting and colouring. Put in the chorizo and cook, tossing occasionally, for 10 minutes until the onions are soft and stained yellow.

Slice the chicken fillets into 3 or 4 pieces. Add to the pan, turning them as they change colour. Halve the salt-preserved lemons, scrape out the seeds and finely slice the skin. Crack, then peel the garlic and slice it into thin rounds. Add the lemon and garlic, chicken stock and rinsed bulgur to the pan. Bring to the boil, reduce the heat, cover and cook gently for 20 to 25 minutes until the stock is absorbed into the bulgur.

Adjust the seasoning. Chop the parsley. Between other jobs, remove the skin of the broad beans. This is quickly done by pinching your thumbnail against your index finger, then squeezing out the bright green bean. Stir the parsley and beans through the pilaff before serving.

23

Fry-ups

Every so often someone asks me where I get my inspiration from, how I come up with new recipes all the time. There's no straight answer, but almost everything, from seeing a fine bunch of parsley to using up what's left in the fridge, seems to get me going. The other morning, for example, when I was bustling in and out of the kitchen, half listening to the serial on *Woman's Hour*, someone mentioned cooking just-picked mushrooms with salami on an open fire. What a delicious idea, I thought, so when I saw salami on sale, I popped some into my basket. The next day, organic mushrooms were on special offer, and as I can never resist a bargain, I bought two packs. Later, when one of my sons breezed in starving, and I happened to have leftover boiled potatoes in the fridge, I found myself making a salami and mushroom hash.

I tend always to have spring onions in the fridge and they gave the hash colour as well as uniting the slippery mushrooms, softened salami and crusted potatoes into one of those moreish, fork-in-the-pan suppers that cries out for a fried egg but would go well with roast chicken or a pork chop, or piled over nutty brown rice. The hash is particularly good made with fennel-seed salami (*finocchiona*) from www.camisa.co.uk.

SALAMI AND MUSHROOM HASH SERVES 2

PREP: 10 MINUTES
COOK: 10 MINUTES

- *125g bunch of spring onions*
- *250g organic mushrooms*
- *8 boiled Anya or other waxy potatoes (400g)*
- *2 tablespoons olive oil*
- *100g sliced garlic salami*
- *salt and freshly ground black pepper*
- *a squeeze of lemon juice*

Keep the vegetables in separate piles. Trim and finely slice the spring onions, including all of the green part. Wipe the mushrooms; cut large ones in half and leave smaller ones whole. Skin the potatoes and cut them into chunks. Heat the oil in a spacious frying or sauté pan over a medium-high heat, add the potatoes and cook until they are crusty.

Reduce the heat and stir in the spring onions, turning them as they soften. After a couple of minutes, peel the salami slices apart directly into the pan. Stir as they wilt and melt, then add the mushrooms. Cook, stirring frequently, for a few minutes until the mushrooms look damp and dark. Season with salt, freshly ground black pepper and a squeeze of lemon juice. Toss again and eat.

The inspiration for these lamb meatballs came from an extraordinary hotel built into the city walls at Taroudant, in Morocco. Authentic local food, as opposed to the international menu, had to be ordered 24 hours in advance, and as I wanted to try everything, meatballs were low on my list. As it turned out they stole the show. It's a useful dish for a party because the quantities are easily scaled up and the dish reheats perfectly, although for the peas to remain bright green, they should be added just before serving. The meatballs are flavoured with cumin and fresh mint and cooked in a thick, aromatic onion gravy sweetened with sultanas and honey, and spiced with Moroccan *ras el hanout*. Serve with a spoon and fork.

MOORISH MEATBALLS WITH MINTED PEAS

SERVES 4, GENEROUSLY

PREP: 30 MINUTES
COOK: 45 MINUTES

- *400g frozen petits pois*
- *2 large onions (400g)*
- *1 tablespoon olive oil*
- *25g butter*
- *2 tablespoons* ras el hanout *with rose petals*
- *1 tablespoon honey*
- *75g golden sultanas*
- *750ml chicken stock*
- *salt and freshly ground black pepper*
- *2 tablespoons fresh breadcrumbs*
- *1 tablespoon sheep's milk yoghurt*
- *25g fresh mint*
- *500g organic minced lamb*
- *2 teaspoons ground cumin*
- *1 lemon*

Tip the peas into a colander and leave in the sink to defrost. Peel and halve the onions; keeping separate piles, finely chop three halves and grate the fourth. Heat the oil and butter in a spacious, lidded frying or sauté pan over a high heat and stir in the chopped onions. Reduce the heat slightly and cook, stirring occasionally, for 15 minutes to colour.

Stir in the *ras el hanout,* honey, sultanas and half the stock. Establish a steady simmer, cover, and cook for 20 minutes. Remove the lid and simmer until the onions are soft, the sultanas plump and the liquid slightly reduced and sauce-like. Add half a teaspoon of salt.

While the sauce cooks, stir the breadcrumbs into the yoghurt. Finely chop about half the mint leaves. Place the lamb in a mixing bowl. Add the breadcrumbs, grated onion, chopped mint, cumin and a generous seasoning of salt and freshly ground black pepper. Mix well with a fork, then mulch together with your hands, forming it into a ball. Pinch off enough meat mixture to roll between wet hands into balls slightly smaller than a walnut. Aim for 40 balls.

Add the remaining stock to the pan, return to a simmer and put in the meatballs. Adjust the heat so the gravy bubbles gently over them: they will darken and firm. Shake the pan occasionally, so that they cook evenly. Allow 8 to 10 minutes. Add the peas and cook until they are tender. Chop the remaining mint. Taste and adjust the seasoning with salt and freshly ground black pepper. Stir in the mint and serve.

Salads

BELUGA LENTILS, BEETROOT,
SAMPHIRE AND ANCHOVY

ASPARAGUS, POTATO,
PEA AND QUINOA SALAD

WATERCRESS TABBOULEH
WITH CHICKEN KEBABS

HORIATIKI GREEK SALAD
WITH AGED FETA

GINGER PRAWNS WITH
VIETNAMESE NOODLE SALAD

POTATO SALAD WITH HERBS

GRILLED HALLOUMI SALAD
WITH AVOCADO AND LIME

WARM PUY LENTILS WITH
POACHED SALMON AND LEEKS

SZECHUAN CHICKEN SALAD
WITH PEANUT AND SESAME

BAVETTE, ARTICHOKE AND
HARICOT SALAD

I love lentil salads and make them often for picnics with hard-boiled eggs and green beans, feta and tomatoes, or pulled ham hock with carrots and a mustard dressing. This, though, is my favourite. It takes minutes to make with boiled beetroots – I usually boil my own and keep them unpeeled, covered, in the fridge – and ready-cooked lentils from a sachet. It looks stupendous.

For me it is the perfect complement of flavours: earthy lentils, sweet beetroot, creamy, glistening lightly pickled Adriatic anchovies and salty, juicy samphire. The salad is simply dressed with lemon juice and the best olive oil you have.

BELUGA LENTILS, BEETROOT, SAMPHIRE AND ANCHOVY SERVES 6

**PREP: 20 MINUTES
COOK: 40 MINUTES**

- *600g small beetroot*
- *salt and freshly ground black pepper*
- *200g samphire*
- *200g Adriatic anchovies*
- *2 x 250g beluga or Puy cooked lentils*
- *2 lemons*
- *6 tablespoons your best olive oil*

Scrub the beetroot, cut off any foliage (young leaves are great in salad, older leaves need to be cooked), leaving a 5cm stalk and the root. Boil them in salted water in a lidded pan until they are just tender. Drain.

As soon as you've got the beetroot on the go, boil the kettle. Pick over the samphire, trimming away any woody ends and roots. Wash it thoroughly, then place it in a bowl and add boiling water to cover. Cover the bowl with a plate and leave until the samphire is *al dente*, checking after 10 minutes. Drain.

Scoop the anchovies out of the packet and separate the fillets; this sounds mad but you will see that most are double fillets. Tip the lentils onto a platter, separating the clumps with a fork. Season with salt and freshly ground black pepper, a squeeze of lemon and a splash of olive oil.

Don your Marigolds to rub off the beetroot skins. Quarter the beetroot and pile it onto the lentils. Squeeze over plenty of lemon juice. Drain the samphire and scatter it over the beetroot. Add the anchovies. Squeeze over the last of the lemon and give the salad a generous swirl of olive oil.

It's agony walking past my allotment neighbour's asparagus bed when the season begins. His spears burst out of the heavily manured soil and keep on coming while the short season lasts. Every last scrap of my shop-bought asparagus goes into this satisfying salad — I even turn the woody ends into a creamy green dressing. New potatoes, preferably Jersey Royals or Cornish earlies, and peas reflect the flavour of asparagus, but to provide bulk without interfering with the flavours, I add a sachet of ready-to-eat white and red quinoa. Couscous would be a good alternative. Quinoa is quick to cook and versatile, like couscous, swelling into pretty little curls after 10 minutes. For vegetarians, in particular, this complete protein, containing eight essential amino acids, rich in Omega 3, 6 and 9, and gluten free, is worth getting to know.

ASPARAGUS, POTATO, PEA AND QUINOA SALAD SERVES 4–6

PREP: 15 MINUTES
COOK: 15 MINUTES

- *250g sachet ready-to-eat quinoa (M&S) or 250g hydrated couscous*
- *250g British asparagus*
- *salt*
- *a generous squeeze of lemon juice*
- *3 tablespoons your best olive oil*
- *200g frozen petits pois*
- *400g Jersey Royal or Cornish early new potatoes*
- *3 tablespoons best olive oil*
- *a generous squeeze of lemon juice*
- *100g feta cheese, optional*

Fill and boil the kettle. Half fill a medium pan with boiling water and, in a bowl, pour the rest over the unopened sachet of quinoa. Holding an asparagus spear in your hands, snap it in two. It will break naturally at the point where it ceases to be tender. Cut the tender spear end in half, horizontally. Trim the pale, tough, woody end of the remaining stalk and slice it very thinly. Rinse and set it aside. Treat all of the asparagus in the same way. Add salt to the boiling water, then drop in the prepared spears. Boil them for 2 minutes, then scoop them into a colander.

Put the asparagus slices into the water and boil for 6 to 8 minutes until they are very tender. Scoop them into the bowl of a food processor with 3 tablespoons of the cooking liquid. Blitz for several minutes with a squeeze of lemon juice until pale and creamy. With the machine running, add the olive oil in a dribble. Pass the sauce through a sieve into a bowl.

Between other jobs, scrape the potatoes. Leave small ones whole and thickly slice larger ones. Rinse, and cook them in the asparagus water. Scoop them into the colander. Put the peas into the water, topping up the pan, if necessary. Cook them until they're tender, then drain. Mix the quinoa, asparagus, peas and potatoes in a shallow bowl. Spoon over the dressing and toss. Add diced feta, or not.

Tabbouleh is a great thing to have on standby in the fridge, perfect on its own or with just about anything from boiled eggs to roast chicken, kebabs, or lamb chops with a dollop of hummus. Traditionally, it is made with phenomenal amounts of flat-leaf parsley, a hint of onion and tomato, the salad jerked into life with lemon juice and a little olive oil. When I didn't have sufficient parsley one day, I used some peppery watercress instead and it proved to be a good addition. Here it's matched with chicken kebabs that go well with the lemon and orange juice vinaigrette. This amount of tabbouleh could be mixed with 400g of cooked prawns or 200g of brown shrimps to make a lovely salad.

WATERCRESS TABBOULEH WITH CHICKEN KEBABS SERVES 4

PREP: 20 MINUTES
COOK: 20 MINUTES

- 8 skinned and boned chicken thigh fillets
- 1 tablespoon lemon juice
- 1 tablespoon olive oil
- 1 teaspoon thyme
- 200g bulgur
- 3 shallots
- 1 lemon
- 25g flat-leaf parsley
- 15 mint leaves
- 85g watercress
- 200g cherry tomatoes
- 4 Little Gem lettuce hearts

for the vinaigrette:
- 1 teaspoon runny honey
- salt
- 1 tablespoon lemon juice
- 2 tablespoons orange juice
- 3 tablespoons olive oil

Boil the kettle. Slice the chicken into small kebab-size chunks. Whisk the lemon juice, olive oil and thyme in a bowl, then stir in the chicken. Stash the bowl in a plastic bag in the fridge.

Wash the bulgur in a sieve until the water runs clear. Place it in a bowl and cover with boiling water. Cover with a stretch of clingfilm and leave it for 20 minutes until swollen but still nutty. Drain it in a sieve, shake it dry and spread it in a mixing bowl to cool.

Finely chop the shallots. Put them into a bowl and mix with the juice from the lemon. Pick the leaves from the parsley and chop them with the mint and watercress. Quarter the cherry tomatoes. Separate the lettuce leaves; rinse and shake them dry. Dissolve the honey and a pinch of salt in a tablespoon of lemon juice, then whisk in the orange juice and olive oil. Stir the shallot mixture, the chopped herbs and tomatoes into the cooling bulgur. Toss thoroughly.

Thread the chicken onto kebab sticks and cook on a barbecue at the white-ash stage or on a hot griddle, turning as the meat forms a crust until it is cooked through. Serve the lettuce dribbled with vinaigrette, topped with the bulgur and the kebabs. This looks pretty arranged on a platter.

There is Greek salad and there is Greek salad. At Harry's beachside taverna at Thanos on Lemnos, all the ingredients are grown in nearby fields. The red onions grow fat and the green capsicums grow thin and twisted but both are sweet and juicy. The flat-leaf parsley is grassy and vibrant, the cucumber delicate and crunchy, the tomatoes intensely flavoured. Every year there is a surprise extra. A couple of years ago it was purple basil with the parsley, another time a few slices of pickled cucumber and the strangest was pickled samphire-like seaweed gathered from the rocks. The onion is sliced in thin wedges, the cucumber peeled, halved and cut into thick pieces and those densely fleshy tomatoes chopped into big wedges. The salad is generous to a fault, packed into the bowl, and dressed with fruity olive oil, a hint of vinegar and one big fat black olive balanced between two huge slabs of oregano-dusted aged feta.

HORIATIKI GREEK SALAD WITH AGED FETA SERVES 4

PREP: 25 MINUTES

- ½ cucumber
- 1 small pale green pepper
- 2 medium red onions
- 4–6 plum or other large, dense tomatoes (750g)
- 1 sweet dill-pickled cucumber
- 4–5 sprigs of flat-leaf parsley
- 4 tablespoons fruity olive oil
- 1 tablespoon wine vinegar
- 200g aged Greek feta cheese
- 1 teaspoon dried oregano
- 4 Kalamata black olives

Greek salads are always packed into the bowl, leaving no room for tossing, so the dressing has to be scooped up from the bottom as the salad is eaten. I prefer to use a larger bowl. Peel the cucumber, halve it lengthways and slice it into irregular chunky pieces. Thinly slice the length of the pepper, discarding the seeds. Peel, halve and slice the onions into slim wedges. Cut out the tomato cores in a pointed plug shape, then slice the tomatoes haphazardly into big chunky pieces.

Chop the pickled cucumber. Coarsely chop the parsley. Pile the tomato, cucumber and onion into a large bowl. Whisk together most of the olive oil and vinegar and pour it over the salad. Scatter big pieces of pickled cucumber over the top and add the parsley. Halve the feta horizontally to make 2 big slabs and wedge them against each other over the salad. Splash with the last of the olive oil, dust with oregano and add the olives.

Here's a dish to wake up your taste-buds. Full of vim and vigour, crunch and slippery noodles, this salad is an unexpected mix of cucumber and fennel with a sharp, zingy dressing. A hint of sweetness comes from using sweet chilli sauce rather than raw chilli. It gives the pale green and white ingredients an injection of red that won't blow your head off.

This herby Vietnamese-style salad is delicious on its own and could be served with any number of things other than prawns: try lime-seasoned strips of fried chicken or fish. The prawns are quickly stir-fried with garlic and ginger, just long enough to change colour and cook through, but not so long that they lose their bouncy juiciness. The finale is crushed peanuts or cashews, but if nuts are off the radar, leave them out. There is plenty going on without them.

GINGER PRAWNS WITH VIETNAMESE NOODLE SALAD SERVES 4

PREP: 25 MINUTES
COOK: 15 MINUTES

- *300g raw peeled prawns*
- *2 cloves of garlic*
- *15g fresh ginger*
- *2 tablespoons vegetable oil*
- *200g vermicelli bean thread or rice noodles*
- *150g cucumber*
- *1 small fennel (150g)*
- *10g fresh coriander*
- *5g small mint leaves*

for the dressing:
- *1 clove of garlic*
- *1 tablespoon Thai fish sauce*
- *2 tablespoons fresh lime juice*
- *1 tablespoon Thai sweet chilli sauce*

for the garnish:
- *2 tablespoons roasted salted peanuts or cashews*
- *1 tablespoon Thai sweet chilli sauce*

Run a knife down the inside curl of the prawns and wipe away the black vein. Peel and chop the garlic; peel and grate the ginger. Crush them together to make a paste, then stir with a tablespoon of the oil. Smear this over the prawns.

To make the salad, soak the noodles in cold water for 10 minutes until they are soft enough to cut into manageable lengths (about 8cm). Drain, cover with boiling water and leave them for 15 minutes to soften. Peel the cucumber and cut it in half lengthways. Use a teaspoon to scrape out the seeds, then slice it into thin half-moons. Trim and halve the fennel lengthways, then slice it thinly. Chop the coriander and the mint. Drain the soft noodles.

Peel, chop and crush the garlic to a paste, then mix it with the remaining dressing ingredients in a large bowl. Add the noodles, stir thoroughly, then mix in the remaining salad ingredients. Place the nuts in a plastic bag, seal the end and bash it with something heavy to turn them into crumbs.

To complete the dish, heat the remaining tablespoon of oil in a non-stick frying pan or wok and stir-fry the prawns, tossing until they are uniformly pink and just cooked through. Give the salad a final toss, pile it onto a serving platter, or in the middle of four plates or bowls, and top with the prawns. Scatter with the nuts and pour over a swirl of sweet chilli sauce.

This potato salad was inspired by *salade cressonnière* in Joël Robuchon's exquisite *Le Meilleur & Le Plus Simple de la Pomme de Terre*, which he wrote in 1993 with Patrick Pierre Sabatier, published in France by Robert Laffont. As my French is menu-talk only, much of the finer detail of the book is lost on me and every so often I have to beg French-speaking friends to translate. The photographs – of his perfect *pommes de terre pont-neuf* (square chips), *gaufrettes* (lattice game chips) and gorgeous-looking gratinées, soups and tarts – are, for me, the most enticing food photography possible. My version of this great chef's watercress potato salad is more homespun than the original but is none the worse for that.

POTATO SALAD WITH HERBS SERVES 4

PREP: 20 MINUTES
COOK: 20 MINUTES

• *1kg small new potatoes*
• *2 medium eggs*
• *salt and freshly ground black pepper*
• *2 shallots*
• *2 tablespoons white wine vinegar*
• *6 tablespoons olive oil*
• *3 tablespoons finely chopped flat-leaf parsley*
• *2 tablespoons finely sliced chives*
• *1 tablespoon finely chopped mint leaves*
• *up to 80g watercress*

Scrub or scrape the potatoes to remove the skin. Place the eggs in the pan with the potatoes. Add half a teaspoon of salt and boil until the potatoes are tender but remove the eggs after 9 minutes. Crack the eggs all over, hold under cold water and peel while they're still hot.

While the potatoes and eggs cook, peel, halve and finely chop the shallots. Place the vinegar in a bowl, season with salt and freshly ground black pepper, and when the salt has dissolved, whisk in the oil, adding a little water to help it emulsify. Stir the shallots into the vinaigrette. Slice the hot potatoes onto a platter. Spoon over the vinaigrette. Leave for a few minutes for the dressing to soak into and flavour the potatoes, then grate the eggs directly over the top.

The dish looks prettiest if you force the eggs through a small hole on the grater but you will have to scratch out the clogged holes with a knife. Season with freshly ground black pepper and a little salt, then pile on the chopped herbs. Gently mix everything together. Now heap the watercress on top. Serve immediately, while the potato is still warm but not hot enough to wilt the watercress.

Snowy white halloumi grills beautifully: the edges are burnished, the texture softened and the flavour released. It needs to be eaten quickly, though, or it turns rubbery, like cooling mozzarella, so have the salad dressed and the cutlery at the ready. The salad is purposely crunchy: shards of chicory and thin slices of fennel with silky roast *piquillo* peppers from a jar bring richness to the flavours and cherry tomatoes sweetness. A few capers and sweet chilli vinaigrette bring zing to each mouthful.

GRILLED HALLOUMI SALAD WITH AVOCADO AND LIME SERVES 4

PREP: 20 MINUTES
COOK: 20 MINUTES

- *6 whole piquillo peppers from a jar*
- *2 fennel bulbs*
- *2 pink or white chicory*
- *10 cherry tomatoes*
- *3½ tablespoons rapeseed oil*
- *3 tablespoons sweet chilli sauce*
- *2 tablespoons lime juice*
- *1 tablespoon capers*
- *2 ripe avocados*
- *2 x 250g blocks of halloumi*
- *1 lime*
- *1 tablespoon chopped flat-leaf parsley*

Slice the peppers into strips. Halve the fennel lengthways, cut out the dense core at the base and slice thinly. Trim the chicory, halve it lengthways and slice the halves lengthways. Cut the pieces in half horizontally. Halve the cherry tomatoes.

Make the vinaigrette by mixing 2 tablespoons of the rapeseed oil, 2 tablespoons of the sweet chilli sauce and 1 tablespoon of lime juice. Mix the peppers, fennel, chicory, tomatoes and capers with the vinaigrette and divide between the plates or tip the salad onto a platter.

Run a knife around the avocados, twist apart and use a teaspoon to remove scoops of the flesh. Toss with a squeeze of lime juice and add to the salad. Cut the halloumi across the width into 8 slices, 1cm thick. Place on a foil-lined grill pan. Smear with some of the remaining rapeseed oil. Put the pan around 4cm from the heat and cook for 4 to 5 minutes until the cheese is burnished at the edges, soft in the middle and juicy. Pile the halloumi onto the salad and spoon over the remaining sweet chilli sauce. Scatter with chopped parsley.

It doesn't take long to cook Puy lentils from scratch and they keep well in the fridge, but I love the convenience of ready-cooked lentils in a sachet. I used a couple for this fresh and healthy, quick and easy warm salad, the sort of dish that works for any occasion, informal or formal. While the salmon and thickly sliced leeks are steamed, the lentils get boil-in-the-bag treatment in the pan down below. This merely warms them through and makes them receptive to a simple red wine and olive oil vinaigrette. The finale is a handful of chopped herbs, either coriander, mint or flat-leaf parsley. The salad is served with a splash of olive oil.

WARM PUY LENTILS WITH POACHED SALMON AND LEEKS SERVES 4

PREP: 15 MINUTES
COOK: 8 MINUTES

- *4 trimmed leeks*
- *4 x 200g fillets of salmon*
- *4 tablespoons your best olive oil*
- *2 x 250g packets of cooked Puy lentils*
- *2 tablespoons red wine vinegar*
- *2 tablespoons chopped coriander, mint, dill or flat-leaf parsley*

Boil the kettle. Slice the leeks into 1.5cm thick rings, then rinse and shake them dry. If necessary, slice the salmon off its skin. Cut it into bite-size chunks and smear with a little oil. Pile the leeks on one side of the steamer and the fish on the other. Cover and steam for 5 to 8 minutes until the leeks are tender and the fish just cooked through.

Warm the lentils by immersing the unopened packets in the boiling water in the steamer pan for a few minutes. Tip the lentils into a mixing bowl and toss with 2 tablespoons of the olive oil and a tablespoon of the vinegar. Add the leeks, salmon and herbs. Toss, and serve piled on a platter or in a shallow bowl with a splash of the remaining oil.

for the stock pot:

• *3 spring onions*

• *4 large cloves of garlic*

• *40g ginger*

• *5cm cinnamon stick*

• *4 star anise*

• *½ teaspoon dried crushed chillies*

• *1 tablespoon toasted sesame oil*

• *2 Lapsang Souchong teabags*

• *600g organic chicken breasts*

• *Kikkoman soy sauce*

for the salad:

• *1 large cucumber*

• *1 teaspoon caster sugar*

• *1 tablespoon rice vinegar*

• *1 red bird's eye chilli*

• *1 large carrot*

• *4 large spring onions*

• *2 small fennel bulbs*

• *100g asparagus tips or*

• *10 mangetout or snow peas*

• *25g coriander*

• *15 small mint leaves*

for the dressing:

• *1 tablespoon smooth
peanut butter*

• *1 tablespoon toasted sesame oil*

• *2 tablespoons sweet chilli sauce*

• *1 tablespoon Thai fish sauce*

• *2 limes*

• *1 tablespoon poaching liquid*

for the garnish:

• *1 tablespoon toasted
sesame seeds*

Variations on bang-bang chicken are among the first things I think to make with leftover chicken, but for a party I cook it from scratch, using the Chinese quick-boil method, leaving the chicken to cool in a highly seasoned Asian stock. This version is a long way from the original.

SZECHUAN CHICKEN SALAD WITH PEANUT AND SESAME SERVES 6

Trim the spring onions and put into a medium-sized lidded pan with the peeled, crushed garlic, thinly sliced unpeeled ginger, cinnamon stick broken in half, the star anise, dried crushed chillies, toasted sesame oil and teabags. Arrange the chicken on top and cover with cold water (around 750ml). Bring slowly to the boil. Boil hard for 3 minutes, then turn off the heat, cover the pan and leave to go cold. This could be done 24 hours in advance.

Use a mandolin or food processor attachment to slice the cucumber wafer-thin. Spread in a colander and dust with 2 teaspoons of salt. Leave for 30 minutes, then rinse, squeeze and pat dry. Dissolve the sugar in the vinegar in a jam jar. Slice the chilli into skinny batons, then into tiny dice. Stir it into the vinegar, then add the cucumber and toss. Cover and chill until required.

For the dressing, place the peanut butter in a bowl over a small pan half filled with boiling water. Stir as it melts, then mix in the toasted sesame oil and sweet chilli sauce until smooth. Gradually beat in the fish sauce, a tablespoon of the lime juice and a tablespoon of the poaching liquid to make a pale pouring sauce. If it is too thick, add extra poaching liquid, adjusting the seasoning with more fish sauce and lime juice. Set it aside but don't refrigerate it; if you have to, place the jar in hot water to melt the solidified dressing.

Return to the salad. Scrape and slice the carrots into very thin strips 8cm long. Trim the spring onions and slice the white and pale green very thinly on the slant. Trim the fennel, halve it lengthways and slice it thinly across the bulb. Slice the asparagus, mangetout or snow peas thinly on the slant. Slice the cooled chicken very thinly. Place all the ingredients in a mixing bowl, add the dressing and cucumber, the sprigs of coriander and the mint leaves, and use your hands to mix thoroughly. Pile it onto a platter and serve scattered with sesame seeds.

The French call it *bavette* and eat it with *frites*. We call it skirt and put it in pasties and pies. Flank steak needs short, sharp or long, slow cooking and it's the former we need for this subtle salad. It's perceived as a main course but could be part of a cold spread with, say, char-griddled red peppers or courgettes, roast aubergines and tomatoes. It's great picnic food. Apart from the steak, sold, incidentally, by butchers rather than supermarkets, and fresh herbs, it's a store-cupboard dish. The creamy little haricot beans are delicious with the Dijon mustard and shallot vinaigrette, and quartered young artichoke hearts from a jar. The salad is perked up with finely chopped flat-leaf parsley and scraps of Moroccan-style salt-preserved lemons.

BAVETTE, ARTICHOKE AND HARICOT SALAD SERVES 4

PREP: 15 MINUTES
COOK: 15 MINUTES

- *2 x 400g tins of haricot beans*
- *500g skirt steak*
- *Maldon sea salt*
- *1 tablespoon vegetable oil*
- *2 salt-preserved lemons*
- *280g jar of quartered artichoke hearts in oil*
- *25g flat-leaf parsley*

for the vinaigrette:
- *1 plump shallot*
- *1 tablespoon wine vinegar*
- *a pinch of sugar*
- *salt and freshly ground black pepper*
- *1 dessertspoon Dijon mustard*
- *100ml vegetable oil*

Tip the beans into a sieve and rinse under cold running water. Leave them to drain. Heat the griddle for several minutes until it is very hot. Oil the steak and season one side generously with sea salt. Press the seasoned side down on the hot griddle and cook it for 3 minutes. Season the exposed side, turn it and repeat. Remove to a board and leave to rest for 10 minutes. Slice thinly across the grain into strips. It will be pink.

To make the vinaigrette, peel and finely dice the shallot. Place it in a mixing bowl, then stir in the vinegar, sugar, salt, freshly ground black pepper and mustard, then beat in the oil gradually, adding a little water at the end to help it emulsify into a thick, creamy vinaigrette.

Finely slice the salt-preserved lemon, removing the pips. Stir the beans into the vinaigrette, then the artichokes, parsley, salt-preserved lemon and steak. Toss well before eating. It looks stunning, as you can see, on a platter to share.

Bakes

SLIPPER AUBERGINE, TOMATO
AND GOAT'S CHEESE

CINTY'S FRENCH FISH PIE

BAKED PROVENÇAL SEA BASS
WITH POTATOES

STICKY PORK RIBS WITH POTATOES

GARLIC CHICKEN *BOULANGÈRE*

GREEK SPRING CHICKEN
WITH LEMON POTATOES

BRAISED CHICKEN, TOULOUSE
SAUSAGES AND WHITE BEANS

HAM AND SPINACH STRATA
WITH GREEN SAUCE

PULLED BELLY PORK SLIDERS
WITH APPLE SAUCE

LANCASHIRE HOTPOT

CUMIN SLOW-ROASTED SHOULDER
OF LAMB WITH COUSCOUS

STEAK AND MUSHROOM COBBLER PIE

ROAST MEATBALLS, SWEET POTATO
AND LEMON COUSCOUS

It's always useful to have a good vegetarian dish up your sleeve and this one appeals to dedicated meat eaters too. The aubergines are halved lengthways, the surface cut with a deep lattice then baked until the flesh is soft and the lattice sagging open. Each is filled with chopped tomatoes mixed with piquant capers and a few scraps of chopped black olive, then covered with thick slices cut from a goat's cheese log. My favourite is Petit Sainte-Maure by Soignon but if that isn't available, choose one you know to have a tangy rather than mild flavour. Baked or grilled to order under a dusting of grated Parmesan, this is a treat by any standard.

SLIPPER AUBERGINE, TOMATO AND GOAT'S CHEESE SERVES 6

PREP: 20 MINUTES
COOK: 35 MINUTES

- *6 medium-sized aubergines*
- *olive oil*
- *16 pitted black olives (Crespo packet)*
- *2 x 400g tins of chopped tomatoes*
- *2 tablespoons capers*
- *2 x 120g goat's cheese logs*
- *freshly grated Parmesan*

Heat the oven to 220°C/gas mark 7. Halve the aubergines lengthways, cutting through the stalk. Use a small, sharp knife to cut a lattice almost to the base but without puncturing the skin. Smear lavishly with olive oil, arrange in a roasting tin and bake for 25 minutes until soft and yielding.

Slice the olives across into thirds. Tip the tomatoes into a sieve to drain, then mix them with the capers and olives. Spoon the tomatoes over the aubergines and cover with thick slices of goat's cheese. Dredge with Parmesan.

Return to the oven or pop under a hot grill to burnish the cheese and heat through the tomato and aubergine. Serve immediately.

Cinty, pronounced Kinty, is the sister of a friend and this is her foolproof recipe. It's as good for one as it is for a dinner party. It's easy to scale up or down. You want plenty of leeks — which are stewed in butter with white wine — then a fillet of white fish per person. I prefer haddock loin but cod, carefully boned hake, brill or lemon sole are good alternatives. The fish is laid over the top of a thick layer of leeks, then covered with a generous layer of full-fat crème fraîche. My contribution is a gratin topping of fine fresh breadcrumbs and finely grated Parmesan to give crunch to every mouthful. It could be made with fennel instead of leeks.

Sometimes when I have plenty of time I salt the fish first. This has the advantage of firming it up, seasoning it and drawing out some of the liquid. For 4 fillets you will need about a tablespoon of flaky Maldon sea salt. Leave them for 20 minutes, then rinse and pat them dry before proceeding.

CINTY'S FRENCH FISH PIE SERVES 4

**PREP: 15 MINUTES
COOK: 40 MINUTES**

- *1kg trimmed leeks*
- *40g butter*
- *salt and freshly ground black pepper*
- *150ml dry white wine*
- *4 thick fillets of skinned haddock loin (approx. 200g each)*
- *300ml full-fat crème fraîche*
- *50g fine white bread-crumbs without crust*
- *2–3 tablespoons finely grated Parmesan*

Halve the leeks lengthways, hold the pieces together and finely slice them into half-moons. Soak them in cold water to loosen any grit, then drain. Heat the oven to 200°C/gas mark 6. Melt the butter in an ovenproof pan to fit the fish fillets snugly, stir in the leeks, season with salt and freshly ground black pepper, cover and cook for 5 to 10 minutes until they are soft.

Add the wine and simmer briskly until the leeks are juicy but not wet. Pat the fish dry and lay it over the leeks. Spread the crème fraîche over the top to cover the fish, then dredge with the breadcrumbs mixed with the Parmesan. Bake for 30 minutes or until the crust is crisp and golden and the fish cooked through.

I like dishes such as this that adapt easily for any number of people and virtually cook themselves. I often make it for a home-alone supper but it's no trouble to scale up for two or more, adding all the ingredients in proportion. Instead of fish fillets, which I have used, it could be made with one or two whole fish if that's easier. It certainly looks dramatic. Black olives and capers, with a splash of olive oil, a few basil leaves and soft, squashy roast cherry tomatoes, give fish and sliced potatoes a taste of the South of France – but this recipe can be used as a template, introducing other flavours, like chopped anchovy with garlic and rosemary, or saffron with tomatoes and green olives for a taste of the Maghreb.

BAKED PROVENÇAL SEA BASS
WITH POTATOES SERVES 4

PREP: 20 MINUTES
COOK: 40 MINUTES

- *2 banana shallots*
- *800g large potatoes*
- *salt and freshly ground black pepper*
- *600ml boiling water*
- *½ chicken stock cube*
- *2 tablespoons olive oil, plus extra to serve*
- *20 pitted black olives (Crespo packet)*
- *2 tablespoons capers*
- *200g cherry tomatoes*
- *4 x 200g fillets of sea bass*
- *a few basil leaves*

Heat the oven to 220°C/gas mark 7. Peel, halve and finely chop the shallots, then put them into a mixing bowl. Peel the potatoes, halve them lengthways and slice thinly, as if you were making thick crisps. Rinse them, and mix with the shallots. Season with salt and freshly ground black pepper. Spread the potato mixture loosely in a shallow ovenproof dish. Smooth the top. Dissolve the stock cube in the boiling water and pour over the stock to almost cover the potato mixture. Splash a little olive oil over the top and bake for 10 minutes.

Reduce the heat to 200°C/gas mark 6 and cook for a further 30 minutes until the potatoes are tender and most of the liquid has been absorbed. Halve the olives and pierce the tomatoes with a sharp knife. Scatter the capers and olives over the potatoes, add the tomatoes and lay the fish, skin side uppermost, over the top. Season with salt and freshly ground black pepper and add the last of the olive oil.

Bake for 6 to 12 more minutes depending on the thickness of the fish fillets. Peel away the skin, or not, and serve in the dish with a flourish of basil leaves and a splash of olive oil.

I find it easier to make this in two medium-sized roasting tins that fit side by side in my oven. Theoretically, the quantities given are ample for four, but there will be no leftovers. I don't bother to marinate the ribs because the intense sweet sour sauce with its hint of chilli and elusive *je ne sais quoi* (pomegranate molasses syrup) combines with finely chopped onions to inject plenty of flavour as the ribs roast. The potatoes wedged between the ribs soak up some of the juices, ending up gooey underneath and crusty on top. By way of contrast, the ribs are very good with a dollop of chilled apple sauce topped with fresh pomegranate seeds.

STICKY PORK RIBS WITH POTATOES SERVES 4

PREP: 20 MINUTES
COOK: 2 HOURS

- *You will need:* two 20 x 30cm x 3cm deep roasting tins
- *2 x 500g rack of pork loin ribs*
- *1 large onion, approx. 200g*
- *2 tablespoons Thai sweet chilli sauce*
- *2 tablespoons red wine vinegar*
- *2 tablespoons tomato ketchup*
- *2 tablespoons pomegranate syrup*
- *2 tablespoons water*
- *1 kg medium sized Charlotte potatoes*
- *2 tablespoons vegetable oil*
- *optional: 250ml jar Bramley apple sauce and 100g fresh pomegranate seeds*

Heat the oven to 180°C/gas mark 4. Slice the ribs apart. Halve, peel and very finely chop the onion. Place in a mixing bowl and add the chilli sauce, vinegar, ketchup, pomegranate syrup and water. Spoon half the mixture down the middle of the two roasting tins. Line up the ribs over the mixture and spoon the rest over the top. Peel the potatoes, halve lengthways, rinse and tuck between the ribs. Season with salt and pepper and dribble the oil over the top. Cover with foil, not allowing any air holes. Cook on a middle shelf of the oven for 90 minutes. Increase the oven temperature to 200°C/gas mark 6. Remove the foil, baste the food with the copious juices and return to the oven for a further 30 minutes until the potatoes are crusty and golden, the ribs charred and the meat flakingly tender, and the juices dark, gooey and sparing. Serve from the tin, with or without apple and fresh pomegranate seeds.

'*Boulangère*' is shorthand for sliced potatoes baked in the oven, usually with a joint of lamb perched on the top. I've made it with various-sized lamb joints, with lamb chops, a whole chicken, whole fish and belly-pork joints, but chicken legs are my current favourite. Remember to add boiling, not cold, water to the sliced potatoes when they go into the oven, and ensure that they are tender before the chicken — or whatever — is added to the pan. The garlicky chicken skin ends up thin and crisp, the fat melting into the moist, juicy meat. It is the potatoes, though, that are the star of the dish. There are never enough.

GARLIC CHICKEN *BOULANGÈRE* SERVES 4

PREP: 30 MINUTES
COOK: 80 MINUTES

• *3 large baking potatoes*
(900g)

• *2 onions (300g)*

• *3 tablespoons finely chopped thyme, rosemary and bay leaves or 3 tablespoons* herbes de Provence

• *salt and freshly ground black pepper*

• *3 new-season cloves of garlic*

• *50g butter*

• *4 chicken legs*

Heat the oven to 220°C/gas mark 7. Boil a full kettle. Peel and halve the potatoes lengthways, then slice thinly as if you were making crisps. Rinse and shake them dry. Peel, halve and finely chop the onions. Choose a pan that can accommodate the thick layer of potatoes with sufficient room to arrange the chicken legs on top. Make layers of potato, onion and herbs, finishing with a flat layer of potato. No need to be too neat about this, but season the potatoes with salt and freshly ground black pepper as you go. Add sufficient boiling water to just cover the potatoes. Cook in the oven for 30 minutes or until some of liquid has been absorbed, the potatoes are tender and the top layer is beginning to crisp and brown.

While that happens, peel and crush the garlic with a pinch of salt to a juicy paste. Work the butter into the garlic. Trim off any excess chicken skin and make several small slashes over each leg. Smear the garlic butter over the skin, working it into the slashes. When the potatoes are ready, snuggle the chicken legs together over the top. Return to the oven for a further 40 minutes until the chicken skin is crisp and golden, and the juices run clear when you pierce the legs with a sharp knife.

Simplicity is the key to so much good Greek food and this way of roasting chicken, with potatoes, onions, lemon, olive oil and white wine, is a case in point. Every time I cook it at home in London, I am wafted back to Lemnos, sitting under a huge olive tree hung with fairy lights, the sea lapping in the distance. At this favourite taverna, they cut up scrawny old boilers, and all the bits — neck, liver, even feet — end up in the pan. They're roasted slowly for hours but my version speeds things up, using tender poussins, or spatchcocked spring chickens. The juices beg for crusty bread. Leftovers are to die for.

GREEK SPRING CHICKEN WITH LEMON POTATOES SERVES 4

PREP: 35 MINUTES
COOK: 60 MINUTES

- olive oil
- 2 red onions
- 2 lemons
- 8 large cloves of garlic
- 900g large waxy potatoes
- 2 teaspoons dried oregano
- salt and freshly ground black pepper
- 250ml dry white wine
- 250ml water
- 4 poussins or spring chickens
- 4 sprays of cherry tomatoes

Heat the oven to 220°C/gas mark 7. Smear a large roasting tin with a little olive oil. Peel the onions, then halve and slice them into wedges. Halve the lemons, and crack the cloves of garlic but don't peel them. Peel the potatoes and slice them thickly. Pour 3 tablespoons of oil into a mixing bowl, add the potatoes, onions, a teaspoon of oregano, salt and freshly ground black pepper. Add the juice of a lemon. Swirl everything around in the bowl to coat it with the oil. Spread the potatoes in the roasting tin, tuck in the garlic, then pour over the wine and water. Put the tin into the oven and roast for 30 minutes.

Using kitchen scissors, cut out each poussin's backbone. Turn the birds over and cut them in half down the breastbone. Add them to the roasting tin. Smear them with olive oil, squeeze over the juice of the second lemon, then season with salt, freshly ground black pepper and the remaining teaspoon of oregano. Roast for 15 minutes. Add the tomatoes and roast for a further 15 minutes.

The potatoes should be tender, some crusty, some gooey, the poussins just cooked and the tomatoes soft. Serve with a share of the pan juices.

This hearty casserole is inspired by *cassoulet*, the garlicky bean stew from south-west France traditionally made with various fresh and preserved meats. In this baked version, chicken thighs and meaty Toulouse sausages are cooked in an aromatic red wine, tomato and onion gravy with creamy haricot beans. It goes down well whatever the weather.

BRAISED CHICKEN, TOULOUSE SAUSAGES AND WHITE BEANS SERVES 4

PREP: 30 MINUTES
COOK: 90 MINUTES

- *6 rashers of smoked streaky bacon*
- *1 tablespoon vegetable oil*
- *6 Toulouse sausages*
- *3 tablespoons olive oil*
- *2 red onions (300g)*
- *1 sprig of rosemary*
- *3 sprigs of thyme*
- *1 bay leaf*
- *2 cloves of garlic*
- *8 free-range chicken thigh fillets*
- *2 tablespoons flour*
- *150ml red wine*
- *300ml chicken stock*
- *400g tin of chopped tomatoes*
- *2 x 400g tins of haricot or butter beans*
- *a squeeze of lemon juice*
- *salt and freshly ground black pepper*
- *25g flat-leaf parsley*

Heat the oven to 170°C/gas mark 3. Slice the bacon into batons. Heat the vegetable oil in a spacious lidded heat- and ovenproof casserole dish over a medium heat. Brown the sausages thoroughly and remove them to a mixing bowl. Wipe out the pan, add a tablespoon of the olive oil and fry the bacon crisp while you peel, halve and slice the onions into half-moons. Tie the herbs together with string. Peel and chop the garlic. Add the onions to the bacon with the herbs. Stir occasionally and cook for about 15 minutes until the onions turn sloppy. Add the garlic, cook for a couple of minutes then tip the contents of the pan over the sausages.

Dust the chicken with the flour. Heat the remaining 2 tablespoons of olive oil in the pan and brown the chicken in batches. Return all the chicken to the pan, then pour in the wine, stirring so that the flour thickens the juices. Let it bubble for a couple of minutes, then add the stock, sausages and onion and simmer, giving the odd stir, for 5 minutes.

Put in the tomatoes, beans, lemon juice, and season generously with salt and freshly ground black pepper. Simmer for a further 5 minutes, give a final stir and remove from the heat. Carefully drape a sheet of baking parchment over the top letting it rest on the food. Catch the edges of the paper with the lid. Cook on a middle shelf in the oven for 60 minutes.

Stir well, taste the juices and adjust the seasoning. Chop the parsley, stir it in and serve.

Here's a great way of making supper from yesterday's loaf. Thin slices of toasted, garlic-rubbed ciabatta or baguette work best, used to sandwich overflowing mounds of spinach and pulled ham hock, the scraps of which are useful for so many dishes. If you can't find it, use any thickly sliced ham and tear it into bite-size pieces.

As the pudding bakes, the Parmesan-flavoured custard swells into the bread, softening the bottom layer but leaving some of the top slices poking through to become crusty and golden. It is very good with a pesto-style sauce.

HAM AND SPINACH STRATA WITH GREEN SAUCE SERVES 4

PREP: 20 MINUTES
COOK: 60 MINUTES

- 12 thin slices ciabatta or 24 thin slices baguette
- 25g butter
- 1 tablespoon olive oil
- 250g young spinach
- 4 eggs
- 200ml Greek yoghurt and 200ml milk or 400ml whole milk
- 40g piece of Parmesan, grated
- nutmeg
- 1 clove of garlic
- 90g pulled ham hock or thick slices of any ham

for the green sauce:
- 3 tablespoons toasted pinenuts
- the leaves from a big pot of basil, at least 75g
- 3 cloves of garlic
- 125ml your best olive oil
- salt and freshly ground black pepper
- 3 tablespoons freshly grated Parmesan

Boil the kettle. Heat the oven to 190°C/gas mark 5. Halve the slices of ciabatta or baguette and spread thinly with butter. Use half the oil to smear a baking sheet and arrange the slices in a single layer. Bake for 10 minutes to dry the bread. Leave to cool. Place the spinach in a bowl and cover it with boiling water from the kettle. Once it has wilted – about 30 seconds – drain, squeeze dry, chop and spread it out to cool.

Crack the eggs into a bowl, whisk them until they're smooth, then incorporate the yoghurt and milk, 2 tablespoons of grated Parmesan and a generous seasoning of nutmeg. Rub one side of the toasts with peeled garlic. Lay half of the toast in a gratin dish in a single layer. Dust it lavishly with half of the remaining Parmesan, top with spinach and ham – torn into bite-size scraps if using slicing ham – then make approximate sandwiches with the rest of the toast. Pour over the custard mixture and dredge with the last of the Parmesan. Bake for 35 to 45 minutes until the custard is set and some of the toast is temptingly crusty. Serve with the green sauce, or not.

To make the green sauce, put the pinenuts, basil, peeled garlic, a tablespoon of the oil, salt and freshly ground black pepper into the bowl of a food processor and blitz, scraping down the inside as necessary. With the motor running, gradually add the remaining oil and continue until nicely amalgamated. Transfer to a bowl and stir in the grated Parmesan. A knob of soft butter stirred in will stop the sauce splitting.

If you are not familiar with 'pulled' as a culinary term, this might sound an odd moniker. It refers to cooking fatty joints like belly pork and lamb shoulder, long and slow so that the fat melts and anoints the meat. This renders it so soft that it can be shredded or pulled apart with two forks. 'Sliders' are small burgers, but this combination of pulled pork, apple sauce and crackling is excellent, too, rolled in a tortilla. With chips on the side, it's a combo made in heaven. It could, incidentally, be made 24 hours in advance, the meat pulled, covered and chilled. The poaching liquid should be strained, cooled and chilled overnight, the fat removed, then leftovers used for soup, risotto or a noodle dish.

PULLED BELLY PORK SLIDERS
WITH APPLE SAUCE SERVES 4–6

PREP: 20 MINUTES (BEGIN
24 HOURS IN ADVANCE)
COOK: 2½ – 3½ HOURS

- 1kg meaty belly pork joint, with or without bones
- 1 tbsp vegetable oil
- 1 tbsp Maldon sea salt
- 2 onions
- 1 carrot
- 4 cloves of garlic
- 750ml cider or apple juice
- 300–500ml chicken stock
- salt and freshly ground black pepper
- 15–20 small crusty rolls
- Dijon, English or American mustard
- 250ml jar Bramley apple sauce
- bunch traditional watercress, such as John Kurd's organic

Heat the oven to 220°C/gas mark 7. Run a sharp cook's knife under the pork skin to remove it in one piece. Score in 1cm wide strips. Rub with oil and sprinkle with the Maldon sea salt. Place on a double thickness sheet of foil and fold the corners to make a square boat to catch the fat as it melts. Alternatively, cheat (you will be using a pan to cook the meat) and place in a small roasting tin.

Peel, halve and slice the onions. Scrape and chop the carrot. Peel the garlic, leaving it whole. Pile the onions, carrot and garlic into a deep roasting tin or Dutch oven and place the joint on top. Pour over the liquid to submerge the meat and cover it with a foil lid. Place the crackling on the bottom shelf and the meat on the middle shelf, then cook for 30 minutes.

Reduce the heat to 200°C/gas mark 6 and cook for 2 to 3 hours, or until the meat is meltingly soft and pulls apart easily with a fork.

Remove the meat from the liquid. Scrape away any fat, and tear the pork apart with two forks, piling it into a container as you go. Spoon over some of the skimmed juices (left overnight, the fat will solidify, or strain into a jug and freeze for about 20 minutes so the fat surfaces and solidifies) and season with salt and freshly ground black pepper. Break up the crackling.

Make the sliders by smearing half a roll with mustard and the apple sauce, pile with pork and watercress, clamp on the lid and eat with crackling on the side.

Everyone has heard of Lancashire hotpot but I wonder how many people have cooked it. Traditionally it is made with lamb neck chops that stand in a special tall pot surrounded by chopped onions and lamb's kidneys, sliced potatoes and water rather than stock, all hidden under a crowning glory of overlapping slices of potato. It is cooked long and slow, filling the house with tantalizing smells that belie the modest ingredients. This version is made in a regular casserole, using neck fillet rather than chops and, even though I say it myself, is superb. It reheats perfectly – in fact, like all stews, it is even better the next day and requires 30 minutes, uncovered, at 170°C/gas mark 3 to heat through and crisp the potatoes.

LANCASHIRE HOTPOT SERVES 4

PREP: 30 MINUTES
COOK: 3 HOURS

- *800g lamb neck fillet*
- *1 tablespoon seasoned flour*
- *3 lamb's kidneys*
- *1 tablespoon vegetable oil*
- *4 onions (400g)*
- *750g large potatoes*
- *1 bay leaf*
- *500ml water*
- *salt*
- *1 tablespoon melted butter or vegetable oil*

Heat the oven to 150°C/gas mark 2. Trim away the excess fat and sinew from the lamb and cut it into 6cm blocks. Halve the pieces lengthways. Toss the lamb in seasoned flour. Dice the kidneys, discarding the skin and white core. Peel, halve and slice the onions thinly.

Melt the lamb fat trimmings in a spacious lidded heat- and ovenproof casserole; if necessary, top up the fat with the vegetable oil. Brown the lamb in batches, transferring it to a plate. Peel the potatoes and cut them into 0.5cm-thick slices. Beginning with the onions, make layers with the lamb, kidneys and potatoes, seasoning as you go, adding the bay leaf and ending with an overlapping layer of potatoes. Pour in the water. Season the potatoes with salt. Cut a piece of baking parchment to cover the casserole, letting it sag to touch the food. Catch and keep it in place with the lid. Cook for 90 minutes.

Increase the oven temperature to 170°C/gas mark 3, remove the lid and smear the potatoes with melted butter or oil. Return to the oven for a further 90 minutes. If the potatoes are not crusty and golden, increase the heat to 180°C/gas mark 4 and cook for a further 30 minutes or until they are.

It is hard to beat the pleasure of sharing a roast dinner, anticipating the feast as the agonizingly delicious aromas swirl around the house. Shoulder of lamb, which tends to be fatty and most people consider difficult to carve, is perfect for slow roasting. I learned to cook it in this desert style in Tunisia, although the flavours remind me of the whole roast lamb stuffed with rice I used to have delivered for parties from the Phoenicia, a wonderful but long-gone Lebanese restaurant where, coincidentally, I met Elizabeth David.

CUMIN SLOW-ROASTED SHOULDER OF LAMB WITH COUSCOUS SERVES 6

PREP: 40 MINUTES
COOK: 5 HOURS

• *You will need: a 24 x 36 x 7cm roasting tin, preferably non-stick*

• *salt and freshly ground black pepper*

• *3 aubergines (800g)*

• *1 x 2kg lamb shoulder*

• *12 cloves of garlic*

• *4 tablespoons olive oil*

• *3 onions (400g)*

• *12 shallots*

• *750g small new potatoes*

• *2 sprigs of rosemary*

• *2 lemons*

• *300ml red wine*

• *200ml water*

• *2 tablespoons ground cumin*

• *100g golden sultanas*

• *175g couscous*

• *450g Woodlands Dairy sheep's yoghurt*

Heat the oven to 190°C/gas mark 5. Dissolve 1 tablespoon of salt in water in a large bowl. Trim the aubergines and halve them lengthways. Hold the halves together and slice across into 4 pieces. Put them into the water and keep them immersed with a plate. Set them aside while you prepare everything else.

Trim any flaps of fat from the joint and make several incisions in the fleshy parts with a small sharp knife. Peel the garlic. Thinly slice 2 cloves and post the slivers into the gashes in the lamb. Finely chop 3 cloves, crush them to a paste with a pinch of salt, then stir it into 2 tablespoons of the olive oil.

Peel, halve and finely slice the onions. Trim off the root end of the shallots, peel and separate the sections leaving the shoot end untrimmed. Mix the remaining cloves of garlic (left whole), the onions, shallots and scrubbed or scraped potatoes in a heavy, deep, preferably non-stick, roasting tin. Add the rosemary and season liberally with salt and freshly ground black pepper. Drain the aubergine, rinse and pat dry and add it to the pan. Zest a lemon in small shirt-button-sized scraps, add to the tin and squeeze both lemons over the vegetables. Add the wine and water and splash with the remaining 2 tablespoons of olive oil. Rub the joint all over with the garlicky oil and dust it with cumin, ensuring the meaty top of the joint is liberally coated. Place the joint, meaty side uppermost, on the vegetables.

Tent the tin with foil and cook for 30 minutes. Reduce the heat to 150°C/gas mark 2 and cook for a further 4 hours. Remove the foil and increase the oven temperature to 220°C/gas mark 7. Scatter the sultanas, then the couscous into the juices around the joint, ensuring that every grain is immersed. Return to the oven for a further 30 to 40 minutes until the cumin is crusty and the couscous hydrated and becoming crusty at the edges of the tin.

Remove the tin from the oven and let the meat rest for 10 minutes. Serve from the tin; the meat can be carved with a spoon. Tip the yoghurt into a bowl and pass it round separately.

Bakes

A cobbler, in the culinary sense, is a rough-and-ready pie, or pastry crust. It's thought to date back to early American settlers who had to improvise with ingredients as well as cooking implements, pots and pans. Skirt steak, recommended here, is extremely lean with a texture that cooks up like loose corduroy. It is very good value and usually sold in one piece. The flavour will be vastly improved if the pie filling is cooked 24 hours in advance, then reheated from cold when the crust is added for the final cooking.

STEAK AND MUSHROOM COBBLER PIE SERVES 6

PREP: 45 MINUTES
COOK: 3 HOURS,
PLUS 24-HOURS REST

- 2 onions (300g)
- 2 tablespoons vegetable oil
- a knob of butter
- 1 bay leaf
- 2–3 sticks of celery (125g)
- 2 carrots (150g)
- salt and freshly ground black pepper
- 1 kg skirt steak or stewing steak
- flour for dusting
- a few sprigs of thyme
- 200ml red wine
- 250g chestnut mushrooms
- 400ml chicken stock
- 2 tablespoons chopped parsley

for the crust:
- 1 beaten egg
- 2 tablespoons cold water
- 200g self-raising flour
- 1 teaspoon baking powder
- 100g packet of prepared suet
- 1 teaspoon finely chopped thyme
- 1 tablespoon milk
- 2 tablespoons finely chopped flat-leaf parsley

Heat the oven to 150°C/gas mark 2. Peel and halve both onions, slice one and chop the other. Heat the oil and butter in a spacious Le Creuset-style lidded pan and gently soften the onion with the bay leaf. Peel and dice the celery and carrot into dolly-mixture-size pieces and stir them into the onion. Season then cover and cook for 5 minutes.

Dice the steak into large kebab-size pieces. Dust with flour. Scoop the onions into a sieve over the pan so that the oil drains back. Increase the heat slightly and brown the steak in batches, removing it to a plate. Return the onions and steak to the pan, then mix thoroughly while adding the thyme and wine. Stir to loosen the flour as it bubbles, then add the wiped, halved mushrooms and stock. It will seem a squash but the mushrooms will soon flop. Bring to the boil, stirring, then turn off the heat. Cut a piece of baking parchment to cover the pan, letting it sag to touch the food. Hold it secure with the lid and trim off the excess. Put the pan into the oven and bake for 2 hours. Take it out, let it cool, then chill overnight.

Heat the oven to 220°C/gas mark 7. To make the crust, whisk together half of the beaten egg with the water. Sift the flour into a bowl, then mix in the baking powder, suet, a pinch of salt and the herbs. Gradually add the egg mixture and work it with the flour into a stiff but elastic dough; you may need a little more water. Chill in a plastic bag for 30 minutes. Pat or roll the pastry to make a thick lid or 6 patties. Place the lid over the steak. Glaze it with the remaining egg, beaten with the milk. Make a central air hole. Bake, uncovered, for 25 to 30 minutes or until the crust is puffy and golden. Serve with a sprinkling of parsley.

71

Bakes

Roasting meatballs can dry them out but if they are made on the large side and the mixture moistened with soaked breadcrumbs or couscous, as these are, they end up succulent and tender. Conveniently, these minced beef meatballs take exactly the same time to roast as chunks of sweet potato and shallots, and the cooking juices are quickly turned into lemon gravy to pour over the top. Served over couscous with a scoop of creamy Greek yoghurt, it's a feast.

ROAST MEATBALLS, SWEET POTATO AND LEMON COUSCOUS SERVES 4

PREP: 30 MINUTES
COOK: 40 MINUTES

- 300ml boiling water
- ½ chicken stock cube
- 200g couscous
- 1 lemon
- 4 tablespoons olive oil
- 1kg sweet potatoes
- 16 shallots
- 500g organic minced beef
- a small handful of flat-leaf parsley
- salt and freshly ground black pepper
- 1 tablespoon Greek yoghurt, and extra to serve

Heat the oven to 200°C/gas mark 6. Boil the kettle. Measure 300ml of boiling water and stir in the stock cube to dissolve. Place the couscous in a jug or bowl, stir in the stock, the juice from half the lemon and a tablespoon of the olive oil. Cover with clingfilm and leave to hydrate.

Peel and chunk the sweet potatoes. Peel the shallots and break them into their natural halves. Crumble the meat into a bowl. Chop the parsley leaves finely. Scatter half over the meat, then season with salt and freshly ground black pepper. Fork up the couscous. Mix 2 tablespoons of the couscous with the tablespoon of Greek yoghurt and add to the mince. Mix and mulch it thoroughly together, then make 32 walnut-size balls and smear them with olive oil. Use most of the remaining oil to smear the sweet potatoes, shallots and a shallow roasting tin.

Put the meatballs and vegetables into the tin and roast for 40 minutes. Fork up the couscous again and pile it onto a platter. Use a fish slice to chase the meatballs and vegetables out of the pan and pile on top of the couscous. Pour the juice from the remaining lemon half and 150ml of water into the pan. Let it bubble until you have a syrupy sauce to pour over the food. Scatter with the remaining parsley, and serve with a dollop of yoghurt.

Big Soups

GREEN MINESTRONE
WITH WATERCRESS PESTO

GAZPACHO ANDALUZ
WITH ALL THE TRIMMINGS

CAVOLO NERO, LENTIL, BEETROOT
AND LEMON SOUP

COD AND PRAWN TOM YAM

PRAWN, FENNEL, NEW
POTATOES AND PEAS

JAPANESE FISH BROTH
WITH BARLEY

MOULES À LA PROVENÇALE

LAST NIGHT'S ROAST CHICKEN
DINNER SOUP

DUCK, PANCETTA AND HARICOT BEANS
WITH *GREMOLATA*

PORK, CHORIZO AND PEAS

POACHED FRANKFURTERS
WITH CARAWAY SAUERKRAUT

MOROCCAN HARIRA

BEETROOT SOUP WITH
CUMIN LAMB MEATBALLS

Minestrone is an excellent fridge-tidying soup. It's essentially diced and sliced vegetables boiled with pasta and dried beans to thicken the broth, so almost anything goes. It's a year-round soup that changes with the seasons and this version is one to make in late spring when the British asparagus season kicks in and early broad beans are available. It could, though, be made with green beans and sprouting broccoli, leeks and chard, and later in the year with carrots and tomatoes. I've cheated with tinned flageolet beans and left out the pasta but I always serve minestrone with freshly grated Parmesan, chunkily cut on a large hole. A spoonful of pesto adds to the flavours.

GREEN MINESTRONE WITH WATERCRESS PESTO SERVES 4

- *salt and freshly ground black pepper*
- *400g podded broad beans*
- *2 shallots*
- *25g butter*
- *150g fennel bulb*
- *125g spring onions*
- *100g asparagus tips*
- *150g courgettes*
- *1 vegetable or chicken stock cube*
- *150g podded peas or frozen petits pois*
- *400g tin of flageolet beans*
- *a handful of young spinach leaves*
- *25g flat-leaf parsley*
- *freshly grated Parmesan, to serve*

for the pesto:
- *3 tablespoons toasted pinenuts*
- *90g watercress*
- *3 cloves of garlic*
- *9 tablespoons your best olive oil*
- *3 tablespoons freshly grated Parmesan*

Bring a litre of salted water to the boil in a spacious pan and add the broad beans. The minute they all rise to the surface, scoop them into a colander and reserve the water in a jug or bowl. Peel and finely chop the shallots and soften them in the empty pan with the butter. Quarter the fennel lengthways, cut out the solid core and slice very thinly across the quarters. Trim and slice the spring onions chunkily. Stir the fennel into the shallots and cook gently, stirring occasionally, while you cut the asparagus into bite-size pieces.

Trim and quarter the courgettes lengthways, then dice them. Stir the spring onions into the shallots and fennel, cook for a couple of minutes to wilt them, then add the reserved cooking water. Crumble in the stock cube. Return the pan to the boil and add the peas, courgettes and asparagus. Boil for 3 minutes until just tender, add the broad beans and rinsed, drained flageolets, then stir in the spinach. When the spinach has wilted, the soup is ready.

Adjust the seasoning with salt and freshly ground black pepper and stir in the chopped parsley. Serve with freshly grated Parmesan and a dollop of pesto.

To make the pesto, put the pinenuts, watercress, peeled garlic, a tablespoon of the olive oil, salt and freshly ground black pepper into the bowl of a food processor and blitz, scraping down the inside as necessary. With the motor running, gradually add the remaining oil and continue until nicely amalgamated. Transfer to a bowl. Stir in the Parmesan.

Not for nothing is gazpacho known as the salad soup: it contains everything you might include in a salad, plus the bread you serve with it and the dressing to pour over the top. It's a peasant soup and suits being a bit rough around the edges. Make it on a hot summer day with juicy new-season garlic, ripe vine tomatoes and extra-sweet pointy Romano red peppers that roast beautifully but don't cause indigestion when eaten raw. I like gazpacho with a full complement of add-ons, the little dishes of finely chopped bits and bobs to pile into the soup that give crunch and vivacity to this tomato nectar. Be sure, though, to serve the soup thoroughly chilled.

GAZPACHO ANDALUZ WITH ALL THE TRIMMINGS SERVES 6–8

PREP: 30 MINUTES, PLUS AT LEAST 4 HOURS, PREFERABLY 24, TO CHILL

- 3 large new-season cloves of garlic
- 150g day-old white bread, preferably sourdough
- 1 cucumber
- 1 red chilli
- 2 red peppers, preferably the pointed Romano type
- 1 red onion
- 1kg ripe tomatoes, including 150g–250g cherry tomatoes
- 2 tablespoons sherry or wine vinegar
- 300ml ice-cold water or ice cubes
- about 20 small mint leaves
- 100ml extra-virgin olive oil, plus 2 tablespoons extra
- salt and freshly ground black pepper
- 3 plum or vine tomatoes
- 1 lemon
- Tabasco

Peel the garlic. Tear the bread into pieces. Place both in the bowl of a food processor and blitz to make fine breadcrumbs. Peel the cucumber. Halve it horizontally and use a teaspoon to scrape out the seeds. Chop half of it roughly. Trim and split the chilli. Scrape out the seeds. Set aside half of one red pepper and chop the rest, discarding the seeds and the white membrane. Peel and halve the onion. Coarsely chop one half and add it to the breadcrumbs with the cucumber, chilli and the chopped red pepper.

Remove the cores in a pointed plug shape from the kilo of tomatoes. Roughly chop the regular ones, leaving the cherry tomatoes whole. Add the tomatoes to the food processor with the vinegar, the ice-cold water (or ice cubes), most of the mint, the 100ml olive oil, half a teaspoon of salt and a generous seasoning of freshly ground black pepper. Blitz for several minutes until thoroughly liquidized. You may need to do this in two batches.

Now prepare the garnishes. Keeping separate piles, finely dice the remaining cucumber and red pepper. Finely chop the remaining red onion. Quarter the plum or vine tomatoes, discard the core and seeds and finely chop the flesh.

Taste the gazpacho and adjust the seasoning with salt, pepper, lemon juice and Tabasco. If you think it needs it – it makes it very creamy – whisk in the extra olive oil. Pass through a sieve, working vigorously with the back of a spoon, to catch the pips and other debris. Scrape underneath so nothing is wasted. Transfer to a serving bowl, cover with a stretch of clingfilm and chill for at least 4 hours.

Here's a new favourite soup combination: earthy beetroot with Puy lentils and black cabbage. Garlic, chilli and sage lift the flavours with a finale of diced tomato providing a bright injection of colour and sharpness. A crumble of Greek feta and a squeeze of lemon give this heartening bowlful a tart, creamy finish. Good with garlic bread.

CAVOLO NERO, LENTIL, BEETROOT AND LEMON SOUP SERVES 4

PREP: 20 MINUTES
COOK: 45 MINUTES

- *200g red onion*
- *20g butter*
- *1 teaspoon olive oil*
- *1 bay leaf*
- *1 teaspoon chopped sage*
- *150g Puy lentils*
- *2 garlic cloves*
- *2 beetroot, approx. 300g*
- *1 unwaxed lemon*
- *1.5 litres veg or chicken stock*
- *1 small red chilli*
- *200g cavolo nero*
- *4 vine tomatoes*
- *100g Greek feta cheese*

Halve, peel and finely chop the onion. Melt the butter in the oil in a spacious, lidded pan over a medium heat. Stir in the onion and cook, stirring often, for about 10 minutes. Stir in the bay leaf, sage, rinsed lentils and finely sliced garlic. Peel and dice the beets. Zest the lemon and add both to the pot with the stock. Establish a gentle simmer, cover the pan and cook for 20 to 30 minutes until lentils and beets are tender. Finely chop the chilli.

Fold over each cavolo nero leaf and cut out the stalk. Slice 1cm wide across the pile of leaves. Immerse the tomatoes in boiling water. Count to 30. Drain, skin and chop. Add the cavolo nero to the pan and boil vigorously for 3 minutes. Adjust the seasoning with salt and lemon juice, stir in the tomato and serve with a crumble of feta.

The hot and sour flavour of the clear, golden broth in this ubiquitous Thai soup acts like a tonic, powering its way through the system, nourishing while nuking germs. This version has more seafood than usual, and potatoes, with beans and mushrooms.

COD AND PRAWN TOM YAM SERVES 4

PREP: 20 MINUTES
COOK: 20 MINUTES

- 1.4 litres light chicken stock
- 4 stalks lemongrass
- 4 kaffir lime leaves
- 25g galangal or ginger
- a small bunch of coriander with roots
- salt
- a pinch of white sugar
- ½ teaspoon dried crushed chillies
- 6 Thai pink shallots
- 400g large salad potatoes
- 200g oyster mushrooms
- 150g fine green beans or 6 Thai long beans
- 3 limes
- 2–4 tablespoons Thai fish sauce
- 4 x 200g thick fillets of cod
- 140g raw peeled Honduran prawns

Put the stock into a spacious lidded pan. Use a pestle and mortar (or something heavy) to bruise the lemongrass. Put the lemongrass, lime leaves, sliced galangal or ginger and rinsed coriander root (saving the leaves and stalks for later) into the pan with a generous pinch of salt, another of white sugar and the crushed chillies. Peel and slice the shallots and add them too. Bring the stock to the boil, reduce the heat and simmer for 15 minutes.

Scrape the potatoes and slice thickly. Add to the pan. Wipe, then halve or quarter the mushrooms. Top and tail the beans and cut into 2cm-long pieces. Add the mushrooms and beans to the pan and simmer for 2 to 3 minutes until the mushrooms are tender, the beans al dente. Stir in the juice from 2 of the limes and 2 tablespoons of the fish sauce. Taste, adding more lime juice or fish sauce, salt or sugar, until you're happy with the seasoning.

Slice the cod across the fillet in 2cm-wide strips. Put the fish and prawns into the pan and cook for 2 to 3 minutes, just long enough for the fish to firm and the prawns to turn pink. Chop the coriander, stalks and all, and add to the soup. Serve immediately in wide bowls with a lime wedge to squeeze over the top.

Everything is cooked in sequence for this pretty — and healthy — meal-in-a-bowl. The cooking begins with potatoes, adding fennel, then peas as the liquid starts to evaporate. There should be just enough to turn the prawns pink, before you add a little tarragon and lot of flat-leaf parsley. A squeeze of lemon finishes off the fresh, zingy flavours. It's only worth making if all the ingredients have plenty of flavour, so that means Jersey Royal, Cornish or other just-dug new potatoes, young fennel and fresh peas or frozen petits pois.

PRAWN, FENNEL, NEW POTATOES AND PEAS SERVES 2–3

PREP: 15 MINUTES
COOK: 20 MINUTES

• *400g Jersey Royal potatoes*
• *salt*
• *3 young fennel bulbs*
• *200g podded peas or frozen petits pois*
• *140g raw peeled Honduran prawns*
• *1 teaspoon chopped tarragon*
• *2 tablespoons chopped flat-leaf parsley*
• *1 lemon*
• *50g Greek feta, optional*

Scrape the potatoes and cut them into equal-sized pieces, leaving small ones whole. Put them into a sauté or similar wide-based pan and just cover them with water, adding a teaspoon of salt. Boil for 5 minutes while you halve and trim the fennel, then slice it thinly. Add it to the pan, pushing it under the water. Boil for 5 minutes, then pop in the peas, shaking them under the water.

Stretch out the prawns, run a knife down the black line inside the curl and swipe it away. Tip the prawns into the pan with the tarragon, reducing the heat and stirring as they turn pink. Scatter over the parsley, add a squeeze of lemon juice and, if liked, a crumble of feta. Serve in bowls with a fork and spoon.

I went through a phase of making my own barley water after a Scottish friend told me how good it is for our general health and well-being. I flavoured it with fresh orange and lemon juice and sweetened it with honey. It looked cloudy and unpromising, and took up a lot of space in the fridge, but it was delicious and stood me in good stead until I discovered cider vinegar and honey (a spoonful of each in boiling water first thing in the morning really does keep aches and pains at bay). Eventually I ran out of things to do with leftover boiled barley but this is one of the dishes that I cook it for specially.

Green nori sprinkle, incidentally, an ingredient required for the broth, is crumbled seaweed; nutritious with a nutty flavour. It is available from health-food shops.

JAPANESE FISH BROTH WITH BARLEY SERVES 4

PREP: 15 MINUTES
COOK: 30 MINUTES

- 60g pearl barley
- 25g dried shiitake mushrooms
- 2 pieces kombu
- 2 trimmed leeks (200g)
- 150g silken tofu
- 4 x 200g fillets of haddock, cod or other firm white fish
- 25g coriander
- 1 carrot
- 2 tablespoons Kikkoman soy sauce
- 2 teaspoons rice or cider vinegar
- 1 teaspoon green nori sprinkle
- 15 pieces of sushi ginger

Simmer the barley in 1½ litres of water for 20 to 30 minutes until tender. Drain it, reserving the water. You should now have 150g cooked barley. Pour some of the barley water over the dried shiitake mushrooms and leave them to hydrate. Drain the mushrooms and slice 1cm wide.

Soak the *kombu* in the last of the barley water, making it up to a litre with cold water, for 20 minutes, then simmer it for 15 minutes until the liquid has reduced to about 600ml. Discard the *kombu* (or keep it to use again in another recipe). Slice the leeks into thick pennies, then agitate them in cold water and drain. Dice the tofu into sugar-lump-size pieces. Cut the fish into bite-size chunks. Chop the coriander. Trim and scrape the carrot, then slice it into thin pennies. Stir the soy sauce, rice or cider vinegar and most of the nori sprinkle into the stock.

Add the drained, hydrated mushrooms, the leeks and carrots. Simmer for about 5 minutes until the leeks are almost cooked, then push the fish under the liquid. Cook for a further 5 minutes. Stir in the sushi ginger and coriander. Place the barley in the bowls, moisten it with hot stock and spoon the fish, tofu and vegetables over the top. Serve sprinkled with the last of the nori, with extra soy and feel virtuous.

Moules marinière with diced fresh tomatoes and a hint of chilli: that exactly sums up this colourful Provençale version of the dish. Serve it with baguette and butter, and a bottle of chilled white or rosé.

The quantities given make a feast for four and a decent bowlful for six.

MOULES À LA PROVENÇALE SERVES 4–6

PREP: 30 MINUTES
COOK: 15 MINUTES

- *2kg mussels*
- *800g large vine tomatoes*
- *3 large cloves of garlic*
- *4 shallots*
- *1 bay leaf or a sprig of thyme*
- *250ml dry white wine*
- *¼ teaspoon dried crushed chillies*
- *3 tablespoons your best olive oil*
- *25g flat-leaf parsley*

Scrub the mussels and rinse in several changes of cold water. Pull off the 'beards', scrape away any barnacles and discard any broken or open mussels that don't close after a sharp tap. Drain thoroughly in a colander.

Place the tomatoes in a bowl, cover with boiling water, count to 30, drain and cut out the core in a pointed plug shape. Remove the skin and quarter the tomatoes. Place a sieve over a bowl, scrape the seeds into the sieve and press through with the back of a spoon to extract maximum juice. Scrape underneath too. Dice the tomato flesh.

Peel and chop the garlic and shallots and place them in a large lidded pan with the bay leaf or thyme and wine. Add the mussels, cover and cook over a high heat for 3 to 4 minutes until all the mussels have opened. Remove the pan from the heat. Scoop the mussels into a warmed bowl, discarding any that are closed.

Add the crushed chillies, diced tomatoes, tomato liquid and olive oil to the cooking liquor in the pan. Bring to the boil over a high heat and cook for 2 minutes. Spoon the sauce over the mussels. Scatter the chopped parsley on top.

PREP: 15 MINUTES
COOK: 30 MINUTES,
PLUS 60 MINUTES FOR
STOCK-MAKING

for the stock:

• *1 roast chicken carcass*

• *1 onion*

• *1 carrot*

• *2 sticks of celery*

• *4 cloves of garlic*

• *a few sprigs of thyme and rosemary*

• *1 bay leaf*

• *1½ litres water*

• *salt and freshly ground black pepper*

for the soup:

• *1 onion*

• *2 cloves of garlic*

• *2 carrots*

• *2 sticks of celery*

• *25g butter*

• *a splash of vegetable oil*

• *a flourishing sprig of rosemary and/or thyme*

• *1 tablespoon flour*

• *150g broken spaghetti*

• *a few boiled potatoes*

• *200g peas*

• *leftover beans, broccoli, cabbage and cauliflower*

• *400g leftover roast chicken*

• *1 lemon*

optional extras:

• *90g pulled ham hock or torn Wiltshire ham*

• *a few chopped peeled tomatoes*

• *25g flat-leaf parsley*

• *2 tablespoons chopped chives*

Here is a great way to get another meal from the remains of a roast chicken dinner. Once the meat has been picked from the bones, the carcass is simmered to make stock. It doesn't take long, and the fresh flavour and nutritious value is worth the effort. The soup is a movable feast, depending on what you have left over, but could be made from scratch. Peas and carrots, chunks of boiled potato, even scraps of bacon, and gravy can all go in, with a fresh input of onion and garlic, aromatic herbs and a handful of pasta.

LAST NIGHT'S ROAST CHICKEN DINNER SOUP SERVES 4

To make the stock, break up the carcass and place it in a pan with the roast chicken debris – other bones, jelly and the roasting herbs. Chop the onion without bothering to peel it, slice the carrot, crack the garlic, chop the celery and add them to the pan. Put in the herbs and the water, which should cover everything. Season, then simmer uncovered for 30 to 60 minutes. Strain the stock, let it cool, and skim it.

To make the soup, peel, halve and finely chop the onion, garlic, raw carrot and celery. Melt the butter in the oil in the stock pot, stir in the onion, garlic, raw carrot, celery, rosemary and/or thyme. Season with salt and freshly ground black pepper and stir-fry for 5 minutes.

Reduce the heat, cover the pan and cook for a further 10 minutes or until the onion is soft and lightly coloured. Stir in the flour until it has disappeared, then pour in the stock, stirring briskly to avoid lumps. Simmer for 5 minutes. Add the broken spaghetti and cook until it is tender.

Put in all the cooked vegetables and chicken, plus the ham and tomatoes, if you're using them. Simmer for a couple of minutes, then adjust the seasoning with salt, freshly ground black pepper and a squeeze of lemon. Chop the parsley and stir it in at the last moment with the chives.

One of my favourite stalls at my local farmers' market (off the A316 just before Chiswick Bridge, in London, on Sunday mornings) specializes in duck, chicken and seasonal feathered and furred game. I often buy duck legs and am always pleasantly surprised by how reasonable they are. The dense, rich meat is great for curries (see page 139) and richly flavoured soupy stews like this that simmer away for hours filling the house with wonderful smells. Serve with a fork and spoon, and crusty bread.

DUCK, PANCETTA AND HARICOT BEANS WITH *GREMOLATA* SERVES 4

PREP: 30 MINUTES
COOK: 3 HOURS

- *400g onions*
- *5 garlic cloves*
- *140g diced pancetta or thin rashers of rindless smoked streaky bacon*
- *½ tablespoon olive oil*
- *4 Gressingham duck legs*
- *salt and freshly ground black pepper*
- *400g tin of chopped tomatoes*
- *300ml white wine*
- *500ml chicken stock*
- *1 bay leaf*
- *3 sprigs of thyme*
- *1 sprig of rosemary*
- *3 large carrots*
- *400g tin of haricot beans*
- *1 lemon*
- *25g flat-leaf parsley*

Peel, halve and finely chop the onions and 4 cloves of the garlic. If using, slice the bacon into lardons. Heat the oil in a spacious, heavy-bottomed, lidded pan and cook the pancetta or bacon until it is crisp and the fat has melted. Scoop it out of the pan and stir in the onions and garlic, adjusting the heat so that they soften and begin to colour.

Trim the excess skin from the duck legs. Season, then move the onion to the side of the pan and brown the duck. Return the pancetta or bacon to the pan, add the tomatoes, white wine and stock, with the herbs tied into a bundle, and simmer for 5 minutes while you peel and thickly slice the carrots. Put them into the pan, then turn the heat very low – a heat diffuser is a good idea here – and drape a sheet of baking parchment over the top, letting it touch the food and holding it in place with the lid. Cook for 2 to 2½ hours, or until the duck is so tender it could slide off the bone.

Rinse and drain the beans. To make the *gremolata*: remove the zest from half the lemon. Finely chop the parsley and the remaining garlic, then chop together the lemon zest, parsley and garlic. Mix it with the beans, then stir them into the pan. Let them heat through, and serve.

Look out for mini chorizo cooking sausages (www.discover-unearthed.com) for this Spanish-style soupy stew. It's one of those feasts that could be expanded with mushrooms and quickly boiled green beans but only needs crusty bread and butter or garlic bread to complete it. It's a good alternative to *chili con carne* but the cooking is far faster.

PORK, CHORIZO AND PEAS SERVES 4

PREP: 30 MINUTES
COOK: 45 MINUTES

- *600g small new potatoes*
- *salt and freshly ground black pepper*
- *1 onion (150g)*
- *2 cloves of garlic*
- *250g mini chorizo cooking sausages*
- *420g free-range pork fillet*
- *2 tablespoons olive oil*
- *400g tin of chopped tomatoes*
- *½ chicken stock cube*
- *200g frozen petits pois*
- *20 basil leaves*
- *25g flat-leaf parsley*

Scrub or scrape the potatoes and boil for 10 minutes in salted water in a spacious lidded pan that can accommodate the entire dish. While the potatoes boil, peel, halve and finely chop the onion. Peel the garlic and slice it thinly into rounds. Cut the links between the sausages and halve them diagonally. Dice the pork into smaller than usual kebab-size pieces. Drain the potatoes.

Soften the onion and garlic in the olive oil in the empty pan. Sear the chorizo in the onions. Add the pork, tossing to brown. Season. Add the tomatoes, then fill the empty tin with water and pour it in too. Crumble the stock cube over the top and simmer, stirring a few times, for 5 minutes. Add the peas, simmer for a further 5 minutes, then return the potatoes to the pan. Chop the herbs. Heat through, check the seasoning, stir in the herbs and serve.

There is something about the bouncy texture and subtly assertive sweet flavour of frankfurters that I really like, although not everyone agrees with me. Here they are poached in a thick soupy stew with bacon, onions and caraway-flavoured sauerkraut, its sharpness mellowed by white wine and chicken stock. With chunks of potato, the result is a hearty meal-in-a-bowl with a good mix of textures and beguiling flavours. It reheats perfectly and is served with a generous garnish of chopped flat-leaf parsley to give colour and freshness. Instead of frankfurters, try this with any meaty sausages.

POACHED FRANKFURTERS WITH CARAWAY SAUERKRAUT SERVES 4

PREP: 20 MINUTES
COOK: 50 MINUTES

- 1 onion (125g)
- ½ tablespoon vegetable oil
- 2 cloves of garlic
- 4 rashers of rindless smoked streaky bacon
- 2 teaspoons caraway seeds
- 350g drained sauerkraut
- 10 x 350g beechwood-smoked frankfurters
- 150ml white wine
- salt and freshly ground black pepper
- 1 chicken stock cube
- 500ml boiling water
- 25g flat-leaf parsley

Peel, halve and finely chop the onion. Soften it in the oil in a spacious, lidded frying or sauté pan over a medium heat. Allow about 10 minutes, stirring occasionally. Peel the garlic and slice it into thin rounds. Chop the bacon. Lightly crush the caraway seeds, rinse the sauerkraut and slice the frankfurters into bite-size chunks, approx. 2cm thick.

Stir the garlic into the onion and cook for a couple of minutes until it is golden at the edges, then add the bacon. Cook, giving the odd stir, for about 5 minutes until the bacon is beginning to crisp, then add the caraway and the rinsed sauerkraut. Stir thoroughly, then pour in the wine and let it bubble into the sauerkraut.

Drop in the frankfurters, a generous seasoning of salt and the stock cube dissolved in the boiling water. Bring back to the boil, reduce the heat slightly, cover and simmer for 30 minutes. Taste the liquid and adjust the seasoning. Serve the soupy stew immediately, or reheat later, with a generous scattering of finely chopped flat-leaf parsley.

Harira is a truly big soup, almost a stew, so thick with lamb and diced vegetables, chickpeas, lentils and vermicelli, it's hard to move a spoon. The broth is flavoured with saffron and tomato, ginger, plenty of coriander and flat-leaf parsley, then finished off with lemon juice for a clean zing to the flavours. The soup-cum-stew is the traditional fast-breaking dish during the holy Muslim month of Ramadan when it is often served with fresh dates. Traditionally all the ingredients are boiled together, but I like to brown the lamb and onions first and cheat with tinned chickpeas.

MOROCCAN HARIRA   SERVES 4–6

PREP: 20 MINUTES
COOK: 40 MINUTES

- 2 medium onions
- 40g butter
- 1 tablespoon olive oil
- 2 sticks of celery heart
- salt and freshly ground black pepper
- 1 teaspoon ground ginger
- ½ teaspoon ground cinnamon
- a generous pinch of saffron
- 500g lamb shoulder or neck fillet
- 400g tin of chopped tomatoes
- 150g brown lentils
- 2 litres cold water
- 400g tin of chickpeas
- a handful of broken vermicelli
- 1 tablespoon flour
- 1 lemon
- 50g coriander
- 50g flat-leaf parsley

Peel and halve the onions; finely slice one and chop the other. Melt half the butter in the olive oil in a spacious pan that can accommodate the whole soup over a medium heat. Add the onions and cook, stirring often, for 10 to 15 minutes until limp and beginning to colour. Finely slice the celery and stir into the onions with half a teaspoon of salt, half a teaspoon of black pepper, the ginger, cinnamon and saffron, and cook for a couple of minutes.

Dice the meat in small cubes. Stir the meat into the onions, continuing to stir until all of the pieces have changed colour. Add the tomatoes and their juice, the rinsed lentils and the water. Bring to the boil, reduce the heat, semi-cover and simmer for 60 minutes. Add the drained, rinsed chickpeas and the vermicelli. Simmer uncovered until the pasta is tender.

Mash the remaining butter with the flour and drop lumps of it into the simmering soup, stirring until velvety. Season with salt, freshly ground black pepper and lemon juice. Chop and stir in the herbs, and serve immediately. If you're reheating it later, chop and stir in the herbs just before serving.

The combination of tender chunks of beetroot, slippery red pepper, onion and peeled cherry tomatoes (don't worry: they're from a tin) in a well-seasoned chicken stock with walnut-sized, purple-stained meatballs is hard to resist. The dish is neither soup nor stew but somewhere in between, thick enough to stand a spoon up in. The earthy flavour of cumin has a surprisingly powerful effect on the meatballs, but coriander, added with the soup ingredients and then later as a garnish, brings another, fresher, dimension to this colourful bowlful.

There is plenty here for four or five gargantuan appetites, but served over green beans, or with crusty bread and butter, or both, it will stretch to six.

BEETROOT SOUP WITH
CUMIN LAMB MEATBALLS SERVES 4–6

PREP: 30 MINUTES
COOK: 45 MINUTES

- 2 onions
- 2 cloves of garlic
- 1 unwaxed lemon
- 2 red bird's eye chillies
- 2 tablespoons vegetable oil
- 2 pointed Romano red peppers
- 500–750g beetroot
- salt and freshly ground black pepper
- 400g tin peeled cherry tomatoes
- 100g bunch of coriander
- 2 chicken stock cubes dissolved in 750ml boiling water
- 400g minced lamb
- 100g couscous
- 1 heaped teaspoon ground cumin
- 1 lemon
- 300ml soured cream

Peel, halve and finely chop the onions. Peel the garlic and chop it finely. Zest the lemon, and finely chop the chillies, discarding the seeds. Heat the oil in a 3-litre heavy-bottomed pan and stir in the onions, garlic, lemon zest and chillies. Cook briskly, stirring occasionally, for about 5 minutes.

Chop the peppers, discarding the membrane and seeds. Peel the beetroot and chop it into sugar-lump-size dice. Stir the peppers into the onions, add half a teaspoon of salt and plenty of freshly ground black pepper. Add the beetroot and, 5 minutes later, the tomatoes. Chop the coriander stalks and add to the pot with the stock. Stir well. Cook, half covered, at a steady simmer for about 20 minutes.

To make the meatballs, place the lamb in a mixing bowl. Chop the coriander leaves. Add the couscous, cumin, half the coriander, half a teaspoon of salt and some freshly ground black pepper. Mix and mulch, then pinch off small lumps and roll firmly between your hands to make walnut-sized balls, transferring them to a plate as you go.

When the beetroot is almost tender, squeeze in half the lemon juice and add the meatballs. Simmer gently for 10 to 15 minutes until they are cooked through. Taste, and adjust the seasoning; you may need more salt. Just before serving, stir in the remaining chopped coriander. Offer the soured cream separately.

Stews

CORNISH FISH STEW
WITH *ROUILLE*

SQUID, CHORIZO
AND CHICKPEA *COCIDO*

SPRING CHICKEN STEW
WITH CARROTS AND PEAS

ARMENIAN CHICKEN
AND AUBERGINE STEW

MOROCCAN CHICKEN AND
BUTTERNUT SQUASH TAGINE

WINTER *NAVARIN* OF LAMB

KOREAN CHICKEN
WITH PEAR SAUCE

PORK *STIFADO*

SAUSAGE AND LENTIL STEW

BEEF STEW WITH PARSLEY, CARROTS
AND THYME DUMPLINGS

VEAL *SPEZZATINO*

Fresh, bright, light and easy to eat with a fork and spoon, this fish stew is Cornish because all the ingredients come from Cornwall. The varieties could be altered — say, sea bass or pollack instead of cod, and sole instead of monkfish, but stick with a mixture and add the firmer varieties to the pot first so that everything is just cooked.

CORNISH FISH STEW WITH *ROUILLE* SERVES 4

PREP: 30 MINUTES
COOK: 35 MINUTES

- *250g podded broad beans*
- *1 onion*
- *4 sticks of celery heart*
- *2 cloves of garlic*
- *1 tablespoon olive oil*
- *a generous pinch of dried crushed chillies*
- *a few sprigs of thyme tied with 1 bay leaf*
- *1 strip of zest from a juicing orange*
- *a generous pinch of saffron stamens*
- *1½ chicken stock cubes dissolved in 1 litre boiling water*
- *500g medium-sized new potatoes*
- *2 vine tomatoes*
- *4 x 200g thick cod fillets*
- *300g monkfish fillet*
- *4 king scallops with coral*
- *8 head-on raw prawns*
- *1 tablespoon chopped flat-leaf parsley*

for the rouille:
- *4 piquillo peppers from a jar*
- *2 large cloves of garlic*
- *1 small red chilli*
- *a pinch of saffron stamens*
- *100–150ml olive oil*
- *4 tablespoons fresh breadcrumbs*

Drop the beans into a lidded casserole or spacious sauté pan of boiling water that can accommodate the entire stew. Scoop them into a colander as they rise to the surface and drain the water. In between other jobs, pinch the rubbery skin of the beans with your thumbnail and squeeze out the green bean. Peel, halve and thinly slice the onion. Slice the celery slightly on the slant, 1cm thick. Peel the garlic and slice it into thin rounds. Heat the oil in the empty bean pan and stir in the onion, celery, garlic and crushed chillies. Cook, stirring often, over a medium heat until limp but hardly coloured.

Add the thyme and bay, the zest, saffron and stock. Simmer gently, partially covered, for 5 minutes. Scrub the potatoes and slice them into thick pennies. Add to the pot. Cook for 10 minutes while you prepare everything else.

Put the tomatoes into a bowl, cover them with boiling water, count to 30, then drain them. Cut out the cores in a pointed plug shape, then peel, halve, scrape away the seeds and chop the tomatoes. Slice across the cod fillets to halve them. Slice the monkfish into kebab-size chunks. Remove the corals and halve the scallops horizontally.

Finish the stew by slipping the monkfish under the hot liquid. Two minutes later add the cod, then, after another 2 minutes, the scallops and prawns. Simmer briefly, just until the prawns change colour. Stir in the tomatoes, broad beans and parsley. Serve with a dollop of *rouille*.

To make the *rouille*, coarsely chop the peppers. Peel and chop the garlic. Trim and split the chilli, scrape away the seeds and chop it finely. Pound, or use a food processor, the peppers, garlic, chilli, saffron and a seasoning of salt and freshly ground black pepper to make a paste. Gradually incorporate the oil to make a gloopy sauce. Stir in the breadcrumbs to thicken it. If the sauce splits, quickly stir in 2 teaspoons of hot stock or soup. Transfer it to a bowl and cover it with clingfilm until required.

I've taken to keeping a bag of cleaned small squid, the tentacles tucked inside the sac, in my freezer. They are fantastic value and perfect for quick or slow meals. The smooth creamy flesh can take subtle seasoning or the full-on assault of garlic, chorizo, red wine and coriander that it gets in this Spanish-inspired stew. The squid ends up soft and silky with a pleasingly gentle fishy taste that is still noticeable despite all the other flavours vying for attention. I love it with crusty bread for dipping and slurping but it's good, too, with separately boiled salad potatoes slipped into the pot right at the end.

SQUID, CHORIZO AND CHICKPEA *COCIDO* SERVES 6

PREP: 20 MINUTES
COOK: 45 MINUTES

- *400g fine green beans*
- *1 chicken stock cube*
- *2 medium onions*
- *4 large cloves of garlic*
- *4 tablespoons olive oil*
- *2 x 400g tins of organic chickpeas*
- *1 kg prepared small squid, tentacles inside the sac*
- *150g whole Iberico chorizo*
- *a large glass of red wine (200ml)*
- *2 x 400g tins of chopped tomatoes*
- *50g bunch of coriander*
- *salt*
- *1 lemon*

to serve:

- *750g boiled salad potatoes or crusty bread*

Boil the kettle. Top, tail and halve the beans. Boil them for 2 minutes in a spacious, heavy-bottomed pan. Measure off 600ml of the water and drain the beans. Dissolve the stock cube in the hot water. Peel, halve and finely slice the onion. Peel and slice the garlic into wafer-thin rounds. Heat the olive oil in the pan over a medium heat and stir in the onion and garlic. Cook, stirring occasionally, for 10 to 15 minutes until the onions are floppy.

Tip the chickpeas into a colander, rinse and shake them dry. Remove the tentacles from the squid sac and trim away any beak (the hard bit under the eyes). Slice the sac lengthways into 3 chunky strips. Run a sharp knife down the side of the chorizo, peel away the skin and slice it into rounds, about the thickness of a pound coin. Stir the chorizo into the onions, cook for a couple of minutes then add the squid strips and tentacles.

Cook gently, stirring continuously for a few minutes, until the squid begins to curl, then pour in the wine. Increase the heat and let it boil, then add the tomatoes and stock. Return to the boil, immediately reduce the heat and leave to simmer gently for 30 minutes.

Chop the coriander. Stir the chickpeas into the stew, reheat and adjust the seasoning with salt and lemon juice. Stir the beans and coriander into the stew. If you're including potatoes, put them in before the beans and coriander and leave them for a few minutes to heat through.

Stews

The glass of white wine in my hand went into this pale, creamy version of *coq au vin*. You need muscly organic chicken thigh fillets, rather than soft, floppy breast, to give good textural interest, with slippery button mushrooms and salty nuggets of pancetta. The dish could be made with trimmed bone-in chicken thighs but I've used fillets and sliced them into double-bite-size pieces. If you choose the first option, allow a slightly longer cooking time. Separately boiled new potatoes and petits pois reheated in the stew turn this old favourite into my idea of the perfect meal-in-a-bowl.

SPRING CHICKEN STEW WITH CARROTS AND PEAS SERVES 4

PREP: 20 MINUTES
COOK: 40 MINUTES

• *750g small new potatoes*

• *salt and freshly ground black pepper*

• *200g petits pois*

• *1 onion (150g)*

• *250g button mushrooms*

• *10g butter*

• *1 tablespoon olive oil*

• *150g cubed pancetta or rindless smoked streaky bacon*

• *6 organic chicken thigh fillets*

• *seasoned flour for dusting*

• *1 garlic clove*

• *1 bay leaf*

• *a sprig of rosemary*

• *2 sprigs of thyme*

• *150ml dry white wine*

• *250ml chicken stock*

• *1 tablespoon finely chopped flat-leaf parsley*

Scrub or scrape the potatoes and cook them in boiling salted water in a spacious sauté or casserole pan. Scoop them out of the water. Cook the peas in the same pan after the potatoes and drain them. Peel and finely chop the onion. Wipe the mushrooms. Melt the butter in the oil in the pan over a low heat. Add the pancetta or bacon and cook, giving the odd stir, until crisp. Now put in the onion and cook, stirring occasionally, for about 10 minutes. Scoop the contents of the pan onto a plate, leaving as much oil behind as possible.

While that is going on, slice down the chicken fillets making 4 even-sized pieces of each one. Dust the chicken with seasoned flour and shake off the excess. Make a bundle with the peeled and split garlic, bay leaf, rosemary and thyme. Brown the chicken in the oil. Return the onion mixture to the pan, spreading it over the browned chicken. Add the mushrooms, tucking them between the gaps, turning them as they change colour. Add the wine and the herb bundle, stirring as it bubbles into and over the chicken. Pour in the stock and cook at a gentle simmer, giving the odd stir, for about 20 minutes or until cooked through. Return the potatoes and peas to the pan and allow them to warm through. Taste and adjust the seasoning. Serve with a sprinkling of chopped parsley.

In Greece they always peel aubergine and I recommend you do too for this subtly flavoured chicken and aubergine stew. It means the aubergine will melt into a creamy almost-sauce imbued with chicken juices. The stew is served over couscous with a dollop of thick creamy yoghurt and a garnish of chopped flat-leaf parsley. The dish reheats perfectly. To make it for four, add a second aubergine and onion, more chicken and a little extra water. A scattering of pomegranate seeds looks dramatic and suits the dish but is an optional extra.

ARMENIAN CHICKEN AND AUBERGINE STEW SERVES 2

PREP: 20 MINUTES
COOK: 45 MINUTES

- 4 skinned organic chicken thighs
- 1 large onion (200g)
- 3 tablespoons olive oil
- salt and freshly ground black pepper
- 1 plump aubergine (200g)
- 75ml water
- 140g sheep's milk yoghurt
- 1 tablespoon finely chopped flat-leaf parsley

for the couscous:

- 150g couscous
- 225ml boiling water
- 1 tablespoon lemon juice
- 1 tablespoon olive oil
- 50g pomegranate seeds, optional

Heat 1 tablespoon of the oil in a spacious, lidded sauté or frying pan and brown the chicken on both sides. If it sticks and resists turning, rest the pan off the heat for a few minutes, then lift with a spatula, turn it and finish cooking. Remove it to a plate. Meanwhile, peel, halve and finely chop the onion.

Heat a second tablespoon of the oil in the pan over a medium heat and add the onion. Cook, stirring regularly, for 5 minutes. Season with salt, reduce the heat, cover and leave to soften while you peel the aubergine. Then quarter it lengthways and, holding the pieces together, cut into kebab-size chunks. Stir the aubergine into the softening onion, place the chicken among the vegetables, add the water and the final tablespoon of olive oil. Cover and cook over a low heat — I use a heat diffuser mat — for 45 minutes, giving the odd stir and turning the chicken once. Serve over the couscous, with a dollop of yoghurt and a garnish of parsley.

To prepare the couscous, stir all of the ingredients, except the pomegranate seeds, together in a bowl. Cover with clingfilm and leave it to hydrate for 20 minutes. Fork it up and serve, with or without the pomegranate garnish.

The mellow flavour of butternut survives powerful Moroccan *ras el hanout*, the spice blend needed for authentic tagines. It ends up meltingly soft, the perfect foil for dense green olives, slivers of chewy preserved lemon and meaty chicken thighs. The gravy is thickened with onion, garlic and coriander. It's a great make-ahead dish, a heartening stew to have on standby, but relatively quick and very easy to prepare. If you are reheating, add the second lot of coriander just before serving. Not only will it deliver fresh flavour but also lifts the look of an otherwise brown dish. Good with crusty bread or couscous to soak up the copious juices.

MOROCCAN CHICKEN AND
BUTTERNUT SQUASH TAGINE SERVES 4

PREP: 30 MINUTES
COOK: 45 MINUTES

• 2 onions (approx. 300g)
• 2 tablespoons olive oil
• 3 cloves of garlic
• 8 organic chicken thighs
• 1 chicken stock cube dissolved in 600ml boiling water
• 4 Moroccan-style salt-preserved lemons
• 3 teaspoons ras el hanout
• 80g bunch of coriander
• 400g diced butternut squash
• 12 pitted green olives

Peel, halve and finely chop the onions. Heat the oil in a tagine, or a spacious, lidded frying or sauté pan, over a medium heat. Put in the onions and cook, stirring occasionally, while you prepare everything else. Peel the garlic and chop it finely. Remove the skin from the chicken thighs and trim away any excess fat. Quarter the lemons and scrape out the pips and pith. Slice the quarters into batons.

Stir the garlic and *ras el hanout* into the semi-cooked onion. Cook, stirring constantly, for a couple of minutes, then add the chicken pieces, pushing the onion aside to make space, spooning it back over the top. Chop the coriander, finely working through the stalks to the top of the bunch. Scatter the stalk part of the bunch over the chicken, with the lemon, tucking in the butternut squash as best you can. Tip in the stock, establish a steady simmer, cover and leave to cook for 30 minutes. Remove the lid, add the olives and simmer uncovered for 10 to 15 minutes before adding the remaining coriander.

The unique thing about this French stew is the haunting sweetness that echoes through the flavours of its rich, dark gravy. It's due in part to stewing the meat gently with lots of sliced onion but also because either meat or vegetables are caramelized in a little sugar. In the spring it's made with new-season lamb, baby onions and purple-tipped *navet* turnips but this heartening autumnal version relies on lamb shoulder, carrots and celeriac to make a harmonious mix of textures and flavours. It looks stupendous served from a large, shallow bowl with a generous garnish of chopped parsley and lightly cooked green beans.

WINTER *NAVARIN* OF LAMB   SERVES 6

PREP: 30 MINUTES
COOK: 90 MINUTES

- *400g green beans*
- *Salt and freshly ground black pepper*
- *1.4kg diced lamb shoulder*
- *2 tablespoons seasoned flour*
- *3 tablespoons olive oil*
- *300g Chantenay carrots*
- *300g celeriac*
- *25g butter*
- *1 teaspoon caster sugar*
- *3 onions (300g)*
- *2 cloves of garlic*
- *a glass of dry white wine*
- *600ml lamb or chicken stock*
- *1 bay leaf*
- *3 sprigs each of thyme and rosemary*
- *1 tablespoon chopped flat-leaf parsley*

Boil a full kettle. Top and tail, halve and cook the beans in salted boiling water for 3 minutes in a spacious, lidded, heavy-bottomed pan, then drain them. Toss the lamb in the seasoned flour. Heat 1½ tablespoons of the olive oil in the pan and quickly brown the lamb in batches. Transfer it to a plate.

Trim and scrub the carrots, then peel and chunk the celeriac. Melt the butter with 50ml water and the sugar in the pan. Add the carrots and celeriac, then turn them to coat them evenly in the butter mixture. Reduce the heat, cover the pan and cook, stirring a couple of times, for 10 minutes until they are almost tender. Tip them into a bowl.

Peel, halve and finely chop the onion. Peel the garlic and crush it to a paste with a pinch of salt. Add the remaining oil to the pan and stir in the onions and garlic with a generous pinch of salt. Cook briskly, stirring often for 5 minutes. Reduce the heat, cover and cook for 10 minutes, until the onion is floppy and juicy. Add the meat, raise the heat and pour in the wine. Stir thoroughly as it bubbles and thickens. Add the stock and the herbs, bundled with string. Simmer, covered, over a very low heat for 60 minutes or until the meat is just tender.

Mix the caramelized vegetables back into the stew, then cover and simmer for 15 minutes. Taste the gravy and adjust the seasoning with salt and freshly ground black pepper. Ten minutes before you are ready to serve, cover the beans with boiling water and leave them to warm through. Drain. Serve the *navarin* topped with parsley and beans.

I once spent a fascinating hour at Leith's School of Food and Wine with Mr Koh, the chef at Kaya, a highly regarded Korean restaurant. I was particularly taken with *galbijjim*, a dish of slow-cook braised short ribs flavoured with pear juice, soy sauce, sugar and toasted sesame oil. Traditionally the dish is finished with chunks of carrot, mooli and water chestnuts, then garnished with scraps of fried egg white and yolk. My adaptation is with chicken thighs, early new potatoes and beans. Instead of fresh pears, I use tinned pears in fruit juice. You will be amazed by how delicious it tastes.

KOREAN CHICKEN WITH PEAR SAUCE SERVES 4

PREP: 15 MINUTES
COOK: 45 MINUTES

- *800g new potatoes*
- *salt and freshly ground black pepper*
- *300g green beans*
- *400g tin of pears in fruit juice*
- *2 tablespoons Kikkoman soy sauce*
- *1 tablespoon toasted sesame oil*
- *300ml cold water*
- *8 chicken thigh fillets*

Top, tail and halve the beans. Boil a full kettle, and use the water, with a pinch of salt, to cook them for 2 minutes in a wide, lidded sauté or flameproof casserole pan. Scoop them out, cool and put aside. Then boil the potatoes in the same pan for 5 minutes. Drain, cool and remove their skin.

Drain the pears and liquidize them with the soy sauce, sesame oil and 300ml of water. Snuggle the chicken into the pan in a single layer and cover with the pear sauce. Season lightly with salt and generously with freshly ground black pepper. Simmer steadily, covered, for 30 minutes. Add the potatoes, cover and cook for about 15 minutes until they are tender. Pile the beans over the top, let them warm through, and serve.

The distinctive feature of Greek *stifado* is plenty of little onions. They bob about in a lusty tomato sauce sweetened with currants and sharpened with red wine vinegar. Although usually a dish for stewing veal or chuck steak, it is good made with wild rabbit (1.4kg cut into 12 pieces) or pork, both of which negate the need to marinate the meat overnight. I use pork cheeks, an excellent overlooked cut that you may have to order from the butcher (definitely from www.donaldrussell.com) and the perfect size for the essential long, slow cooking. Like most stews and soups, it is best made one day and eaten the next so that the flavours have a chance to mature and mellow. Serve with crusty bread and butter to mop up the delicious juices.

PORK *STIFADO* SERVES 4

PREP: 25 MINUTES
COOK: 1 HOUR 45 MINUTES

- *20 pickling onions*
- *750g pork cheeks or pork shoulder steaks*
- *8 cloves of garlic*
- *1 bay leaf*
- *a sprig of rosemary*
- *2 sprigs of thyme*
- *3 tablespoons olive oil*
- *350ml red wine*
- *500ml passata*
- *1 tablespoon tomato purée*
- *3 tablespoons red wine vinegar*
- *2 tablespoons sultanas or currants*
- *salt and freshly ground black pepper*

Cover the unpeeled onions with water and boil them in a flameproof, lidded casserole pan for 2 minutes. Drain, let them cool, then peel. Cut a cross in the root end to avoid the middle slipping out as they stew. Leave pork cheeks whole and cut shoulder steaks into double-bite-size pieces. Peel the garlic and leave it whole. Bundle the herbs together and tie them with kitchen string.

Heat the oil in the pan and brown the meat in batches, transferring it to a plate as you go. Drain the excess oil from the pan, return the meat to it, then add the garlic and red wine. Bubble for a couple of minutes, scraping up any crusty bits. Reduce the heat and add the passata, tomato purée, vinegar and herb bundle. Tuck the onions under the liquid, reduce the heat, cover and simmer for 45 minutes.

Add the sultanas or currants, give the stew a stir, partially cover the pan and simmer for a further 45 minutes until the gravy is thick and the meat very tender. Add a little water if it seems dry and cook for a little longer if the meat is not ready. Alternatively, cook, covered, for 3 hours at 150°C/gas mark 2. Taste, then season with salt and freshly ground black pepper.

Sausages and lentils are a combination made in heaven and for this way of combining them you must buy decent meaty pork sausages. They are cooked first in the pan, then halved on the slant and stirred into green Puy lentils cooked gently with carrot, onion and garlic. A hint of chilli and a squeeze of lemon right at the end of cooking give the lentils a hit of excitement while parsley brightens the look of the dish giving it a grassy finish. If it is easier, the sausages could be oiled and cooked in the oven – 30 minutes at 200°C/gas mark 6 – while the lentils cook. But that means breaking the rule of this book.

SAUSAGE AND LENTIL STEW SERVES 4

PREP: 20 MINUTES
COOK: 60 MINUTES

- 3 tablespoons olive oil
- 12 meaty pork sausages
- 1 onion (100g)
- 2 cloves of garlic
- 2 carrots (200g)
- a generous pinch of dried crushed chillies
- 300g Puy lentils
- 900ml water
- ½ chicken stock cube
- salt and freshly ground black pepper
- 2 tablespoons chopped flat-leaf parsley

to serve:

- 1 lemon
- Dijon mustard

Heat a tablespoon of the oil in a spacious lidded sauté or frying pan, and fry the sausages until they're done to your liking. Transfer them to a plate and wash the pan. Peel, halve and finely chop the onion; peel and chop the garlic. Scrape the carrots and chop them into dolly-mixture-size dice.

Heat another tablespoon of the oil in the pan, then stir in the onion and garlic. After 5 minutes add the carrot and continue to cook, stirring often, for a further 5 minutes. Add the crushed chillies, lentils and water, then crumble in the stock cube. Bring to the boil, stirring to dissolve the stock cube, then reduce the heat. Cover the pan and simmer for 30 minutes or until the lentils are tender and most of the liquid has been absorbed. Leave covered for 5 minutes, then season the lentils with salt and freshly ground black pepper to taste, stir in half the flat-leaf parsley and the final tablespoon of olive oil.

Halve the sausages on the slant, stir them through the hot sloppy lentils and gently reheat. Serve with a lemon wedge to squeeze over the top and the pot of Dijon mustard.

It's always difficult to gauge the thickness and amount of liquid for a stew. I tend to flour, then fry the meat before I add any liquid, but if the gravy doesn't end up thick enough, and I like it thick and luscious, I stir in pellets of flour worked into butter right at the end. This quick fix results in creamy, glossy gravy, and I like plenty of it so that leftovers can be poured over a thick slice of bread the next day. Stew, like many soups, is always better the next day but sometimes we can't wait.

BEEF STEW WITH PARSLEY, CARROTS AND THYME DUMPLINGS SERVES 4

PREP: 30 MINUTES
COOK: 2 HOURS

- *1kg chuck steak*
- *2 tablespoons flour*
- *3 tablespoons vegetable oil*
- *2 onions (300g)*
- *1 carrot*
- *1 stick of celery*
- *1 bay leaf*
- *2 sprigs each of rosemary and thyme*
- *3 anchovies in oil, chopped, or 1 tablespoon anchovy essence*
- *150ml red wine*
- *400ml stock*
- *salt and freshly ground black pepper*
- *500g Chantenay carrots*
- *50g flat-leaf parsley*

for the dumplings:
- *100g self-raising flour*
- *50g Atora shredded suet*
- *2 teaspoons finely chopped thyme*
- *4–5 tablespoons cold water*
- *salt and freshly ground black pepper*

Cut the steak into double-bite-size pieces and dust with seasoned flour. Heat 2 tablespoons of the oil in a spacious lidded flameproof casserole that can accommodate the entire stew, and fry the meat in batches. Cook until it is crusty, transferring it to a plate as you go.

Peel, halve and finely chop the onions. Scrape and finely chop the carrot and celery. Soften all three in the remaining tablespoon of oil in the casserole. Bury the bay, rosemary and thyme, tied in a bundle, in their midst. Tip the meat and the juices over the vegetables, adding the chopped anchovies or anchovy essence. Cover and cook for 5 minutes, then pour in the wine, letting it bubble up, stirring so the flour on the meat is knocked off into the juices to thicken it.

Pour in the stock, stirring as it comes to the boil. Taste and adjust the seasoning with salt and freshly ground black pepper. Reduce the heat immediately, drape a piece of greaseproof paper over the pan, touching the food, then cover tightly with the lid and cook very gently for 90 minutes.

Trim the Chantenay carrots and chop the parsley leaves. Make the dumplings by mixing together the sifted flour, suet and thyme with a very generous seasoning of salt and freshly ground black pepper. Use a fork to incorporate sufficient water to make a firm but pliable dough. With floured fingers, form it into 16 marble-sized balls.

Add the carrots and half of the parsley to the stew, pushing them under the gravy. Put in the dumplings, cover and cook for a further 30 minutes until the meat is very tender and the dumplings puffed and fluffy. Serve straight away, or reheat tomorrow, adding extra parsley.

117

A last-minute garnish of finely chopped lemon zest and flat-leaf parsley does wonders for this simple yet simply delicious Italian stew. A friend came across the recipe while doing research for oven-makers Bertazzoni in Guastalla, near Parma. *Spezzatino* simply means 'stew' (*spezzare* means 'to cut', so literally *spezzatino* means 'cut small'). My version is blessedly modest, seasoned with a hint of rosemary, chopped carrot, celery and onion, white wine and water or light chicken stock. It is served over polenta, which is slackened with Parmesan and butter, then finished with a zesty parsley garnish and more grated Parmesan. Look out for British rose veal or make it with stewing steak which is likely to require slightly longer cooking.

VEAL *SPEZZATINO* SERVES 4

PREP: 30 MINUTES
COOK: 60–90 MINUTES

- *1kg lean stewing veal or 1kg trimmed shin or chuck steak*
- *flour for dusting*
- *3–4 tablespoons olive oil*
- *1 medium onion*
- *1 large carrot*
- *1 fennel bulb*
- *1 sprig of rosemary*
- *200ml dry white wine*
- *350ml light chicken stock or water*
- *salt and freshly ground black pepper*
- *25g flat-leaf parsley*
- *1 large unwaxed lemon*
- *250g quick-cook polenta*
- *800ml boiling water*
- *50g butter*
- *50g grated Parmesan, with extra for serving*

Cut the meat into large kebab-size pieces. Dust them with flour, shaking off the excess. Heat 2 tablespoons of the oil in a spacious heavy-bottomed, lidded pan that can accommodate the stew, then brown the meat in batches. Transfer it to a plate as you go.

Peel, halve and finely chop the onion. Scrape, trim and chop the carrot into dolly-mixture-size dice. Chop the fennel to the same size. Strip the rosemary leaves from the stalk and chop them to dust. When the meat is done, put 1½ tablespoons of the oil into the pan and add the onion and rosemary, tossing them around for a few minutes. Drop in the carrot and fennel. Stir, cover and cook gently for 5 minutes.

Return the meat to the pan and mix it into the semi-cooked vegetables. Pour in the wine, stirring as it bubbles away, then add the stock. Season lightly with salt and freshly ground black pepper, cover and cook at a steady simmer for 90 minutes or until the meat is very tender. Finely chop the flat-leaf parsley. Zest the lemon, chop it, then chop again with the parsley to mix.

When you're ready to serve, tip the stew into a warmed serving bowl. Keep it warm while you cook the polenta. Boil a full kettle while you wash the pan. Stir the polenta into 800ml salted boiling water, stirring for a minute or two until it thickens. Stir in the butter and Parmesan until they have dissolved.

Serve the polenta in the middle of hot plates topped with stew, then strew it with the parsley and lemon zest garnish and some extra Parmesan.

Curries

COCONUT EGG MASALA
WITH NAAN

AROMATIC HINDU LAMB CURRY
WITH TOMATOES

AUBERGINE CURRY

LEEK AND POTATO CURRY
WITH SMOKED FISH

MUMBAI PRAWN PASTA

SALMON AND TOMATO CURRY

SAFFRON CHICKEN WITH APRICOTS
AND CARDAMOM

THAI TOMATO CHICKEN CURRY
WITH NOODLES

SRI LANKAN CHICKEN CURRY WITH
SWEET POTATO AND SPINACH

THAI DUCK AND POTATO CURRY
WITH CUCUMBER RELISH

Not only is this curry easy to make, it tastes and looks like a posh Indian takeaway, particularly if there is fresh coriander on hand, plus a jar of mango and/or lime chutney, creamy yoghurt, and crusty naan bread to scoop it up with. My latest variation to this favourite curry is creamed coconut. It's available now in useful 50g sachets and one is enough to soften all the flavours and make a creamier, more cohesive sauce. Cooked prawns would be a good alternative to eggs: just stir them in right at the end to warm through.

COCONUT EGG MASALA WITH NAAN SERVES 4

PREP: 30 MINUTES
COOK: 45 MINUTES

• *3 large onions (600g)*
• *2 tablespoons vegetable oil*
• *6 vine tomatoes (750g) or 2 x 400g tins of chopped tomatoes*
• *6 cardamom pods*
• *1 teaspoon coriander seeds*
• *1 teaspoon cumin seeds*
• *½ teaspoon black peppercorns*
• *½ teaspoon cayenne pepper or dried crushed chillies*
• *4 cloves of garlic*
• *50g fresh ginger*
• *1 teaspoon turmeric*
• *salt*
• *50g sachet of creamed coconut*
• *1 lemon*
• *8 hard-boiled eggs*
• *a few sprigs of coriander*

to serve:

• *yoghurt*
• *lime and/or mango chutney*
• *4 naan*

Peel, halve and finely chop the onions. Heat the oil in a spacious sauté pan or wok over a medium-high heat. Stir in the onions and cook, tossing regularly, for about 20 minutes until they are turning brown but not scorched. If using fresh tomatoes put them into a bowl, cover with boiling water, count to 30, drain and cut out the cores in a pointed plug shape. Peel and quarter the tomatoes. Place a sieve over another bowl and scrape the seeds into it. Press down to extract the maximum liquid; you should get about 4 tablespoons. Dice the tomato flesh.

Crack the cardamom pods and extract the seeds. Crush them with the coriander seeds, cumin, peppercorns and cayenne pepper or chillies to make a coarse powder. Peel the garlic and ginger. Coarsely chop both, then pound with the spices to make a smooth masala paste. I do this using a stick blender, adding the tomato liquid to make the grinding easier. Stir the masala paste and turmeric into the onions and stir-fry for a couple of minutes. Add the tomatoes and a generous pinch of salt. Simmer vigorously, stirring occasionally, for 10 to 15 minutes until the sauce begins to thicken. Dissolve the creamed coconut in 200ml boiling water and add to the pan. Simmer for a few minutes until it has thickened. Season to taste with salt and lemon juice.

Peel the boiled eggs (previously cooked in the pan, obviously) under running water and halve them lengthways. Coarsely chop the coriander, then stir most of it through the hot sauce. Arrange the eggs, sunny side up, in the sauce. Scatter over the last of the coriander, and serve with yoghurt, lime and/or mango chutney, and hot naan for scooping.

for the tomato gravy:
• *600g vine tomatoes*
• *2 tablespoons vegetable oil*
• *4 cloves*
• *1 cardamom pod*

for the curry:
• *8 red onions (600g)*
• *3 tablespoons vegetable oil*
• *2 bay leaves*
• *4 cardamom pods*
• *4 cloves*
• *9 cloves of garlic*
• *30g ginger*
• *1kg diced lamb leg steaks*
• *2 teaspoons salt*
• *3 tablespoons chopped coriander*

for the coriander mint sauce:
• *50g coriander leaves*
• *50g mint leaves*
• *1 clove of garlic*
• *2 small green bird's eye chillies*
• *1 tablespoon lime juice*
• *½ teaspoon white sugar*
• *½ teaspoon salt*

to serve:
• *450g Woodlands sheep's yoghurt*

My copy of Christine Mansfield's stunningly beautiful *Tasting India* is littered with yellow stickers. When I had friends over for dinner and wanted a make-ahead meal, I liked the sound of a Maharashtrian Hindu recipe with tomatoes and mutton, and decided to adapt it with lamb. Since then I have cooked my version again and again. It is aromatic rather than hot, and I begin by making the fresh tomato gravy, flavoured with cloves and cardamom, that provides the liquid for the curry. More cloves and cardamom, quite a lot of gently softened red onion, garlic and ginger and a couple of bay leaves provide a surprising amount of flavour. This is very good with a fearsomely hot mint and coriander relish-cum-sauce, creamy yoghurt and Indian bread for scooping.

AROMATIC HINDU LAMB CURRY WITH TOMATOES SERVES 4–6

Start with the gravy. Quarter the tomatoes. Heat the oil in a spacious, lidded sauté pan over a medium heat and stir-fry the cloves and lightly crushed cardamom pod for a minute until fragrant. Stir in the tomatoes and cook, covered, over a low heat for 30 minutes until very soft. Pass the spicy tomatoes through a sieve and discard the seeds, skin etc.

To make the curry, peel, halve and finely slice the onions. Heat the oil in the clean pan over medium-low heat and stir-fry the bay, crushed cardamom pods and cloves for a minute until fragrant. Stir in the onion. Peel and grate or finely chop the garlic and ginger. Add them to the pan and cook, covered, for 10 minutes, giving an occasional stir.

When the mixture is pale and sloppy, add the meat, stirring to combine. Cover and cook over a low heat for 10 minutes or until the meat is very juicy. Add the tomato gravy and the salt, then cover and simmer for 40 minutes or until the meat is tender. Check the seasoning. Just before serving, stir through the coriander.

To make the coriander mint sauce: blitz all the ingredients, adding extra sugar and salt to taste, until you have a smooth sauce. Serve it with the curry.

Aubergines love spicy flavours. Here, it's gently curried and cooked until slippery soft with onion, garlic, ginger and tomatoes. I've taken the lazy route, using curry powder, but you may prefer to roast and grind your own curry mix. The flavours are sharpened with cayenne pepper, and get a final curry-boost from garam masala. The best, unless you grind your own, comes in a mill (www.bart-ingredients. co.uk). Serve the curry with coriander leaves and creamy yoghurt. Good with hot naan bread for scooping, or roll it up in chapatis.

AUBERGINE CURRY SERVES 4

PREP: 20 MINUTES
COOK: 45 MINUTES

- 2 medium aubergines (250g each)
- 1 tablespoon salt
- 2 onions (175g)
- 2 large cloves of garlic, preferably new season
- 30g ginger
- 400g tin of chopped tomatoes or 800g fresh tomatoes
- 3 tablespoons vegetable oil
- 1 tablespoon curry powder
- ¼ teaspoon cayenne pepper
- salt and freshly ground black pepper
- 1 tablespoon garam masala
- a few sprigs of coriander
- 4 tablespoons sheep's milk yoghurt

Trim the aubergines and quarter them lengthways. Then hold them together and slice across into large bite-size chunks. Place in a mixing bowl. Add the tablespoon of salt and cover them with water. Use a saucepan lid or plate to keep the aubergines immersed. Leave for at least 20 minutes while you prepare everything else.

Peel, halve and chop the onion. Peel the garlic and chop it coarsely. Peel the ginger, slice it into batons, then chop them into small scraps. If using fresh tomatoes, cover them with boiling water, count to 30, then drain and cut out the cores in a pointed plug shape. Peel and chop the tomatoes.

Heat a wok and swirl the oil around the surface. Add the onion and garlic, then stir-fry for 5 minutes. Quickly rinse and drain the aubergine, pat it dry and add it to the onions. Keep tossing for a further 10-15 minutes until the aubergine begins to wilt and soften. Reduce the heat slightly, then sprinkle the curry powder and cayenne pepper over the top and toss for another couple of minutes.

Add the ginger and the tomatoes. If you're using tinned tomatoes, fill the tin with water and pour it in. With fresh tomatoes, add 150ml of water. Simmer, giving the occasional stir, for 20 to 30 minutes until the aubergine is soft and gooey and the juices are thick. Taste and adjust the seasoning with salt and freshly ground black pepper. Stir in the garam masala. Scatter over the chopped coriander and serve with a dollop of yoghurt. This dish reheats perfectly.

Instead of smoked haddock, you could use smoked cod or hake – two new lines at my fishmonger's – for this quick and simple after-work curry. Thick slices of the pale, creamy fish look stunning over the saffron-coloured gravy with specks of bright red chilli poking through. The sweetness of mango chutney goes particularly well with this dish.

LEEK AND POTATO CURRY
WITH SMOKED FISH SERVES 2

PREP: 20 MINUTES
COOK: 35 MINUTES

- 2 medium onions
- 1 tablespoon vegetable oil
- 2 trimmed leeks (175g)
- 2 small dried red chillies
- 2 cloves of garlic
- salt
- 2 Marfona or other dense-fleshed potatoes (300g)
- 3 teaspoons curry powder
- 400ml water
- 300g naturally smoked haddock
- a few leaves of fresh mint and coriander

to serve:

- mango chutney
- 1 lime

Peel, halve and thinly slice the onions. Heat the oil in a lidded sauté pan, stir in the onions and let them soften for a few minutes, giving the occasional stir; you want them pale and uncoloured. Meanwhile, slice the leeks into 1cm-thick pennies; wash and shake them dry. Quarter the chillies lengthways, scrape away the seeds and slice them into skinny batons, then into tiny dice. Peel the garlic and slice it into thin rounds. Stir the leeks, chilli and garlic into the softening onions and season lavishly with salt. Cover and cook for 5 minutes. Stir, then continue to cook for a further 5 minutes.

Peel the potatoes and slice them 0.5cm thick. Don't rinse them: the starch will help to thicken the curry. Stir the curry powder into the vegetables and cook, stirring, for a couple of minutes to cook the spices. Pour in the water. Submerge the potatoes, establish a gentle simmer, cover and cook for about 10 minutes or until they are tender to the point of a knife. Check the seasoning: you may need more salt but don't overdo it.

Slice the fish off the skin and cut across the width of the fillets into 1.5cm thick slices. When the potatoes are tender, lay the fish over the top, cover again and leave for a further 3 to 8 minutes until it is just cooked. Scatter the chopped herbs over the top. Serve with mango chutney and a lime wedge.

It's a bit cheeky calling this a Mumbai dish because the link is tenuous in the extreme. It is, though, extraordinarily delicious and super-quick to cook, delivering a gentle hint of curry and surprisingly complex flavours. There isn't a sauce as such, just noodle cooking water mixed into the curry paste with onion and garlic. That might not sound very promising but the result is a surprisingly creamy, slurpy deliciousness, the golden noodles uplifted by the freshness of the tomatoes and vibrant green herbs. Bobbing between the noodles, flashes of pink prawns give each mouthful a sweetness and textural contrast to all the softness.

MUMBAI PRAWN PASTA SERVES 2, GENEROUSLY

PREP: 15 MINUTES
COOK: 20 MINUTES

• 1 onion (75g)

• 1 clove of garlic

• salt

• 2 tablespoons vegetable oil

• 275g bag of cooked
fine egg noodles

• 2 large vine tomatoes (250g)

• 200g raw peeled king prawns

• 2 teaspoons curry powder

• 25g coriander

• 10 mint leaves

• 1 lemon

Peel, halve and finely chop the onion. Peel the garlic, then crush it to a paste with a pinch of salt. Heat the oil in a spacious frying or sauté pan and gently soften the onion, stirring in the crushed garlic 5 minutes later. Meanwhile, place the noodles in a bowl and cover with boiling water to heat through. Drain, reserving 200ml of the cooking water. Cover the noodles with clingfilm to keep warm.

Put the tomatoes into a bowl, cover it with boiling water, count to 30, then drain and cut out the core in a pointed plug shape. Peel and quarter the tomatoes, then chop the flesh. Run a knife down the inside curl of the prawns and scrape away the black line. Add the curry powder to the softened onion, stir-frying for 30 seconds, then tip in the tomato and 50ml of the noodle cooking liquid. Simmer briskly for 5 minutes while you chop the coriander and mint leaves.

Add the prawns, tossing as they change colour, then pour in the rest of the reserved cooking water and the lemon juice. Stir in the herbs and the noodles, and continue for a couple of minutes to mix and merge until the curry is juicy rather than wet. Any leftovers are good cold.

Tomatoes take to curry deliciously well. I was slow to work out how well they go with salmon too, and as this oily fish, like mackerel, can take strong flavouring, particularly curry, putting the two together seemed a good idea. The result is a quick, fragrant curry with a lemony coconut gravy. Coriander accentuates the lovely colour and the fresh, light flavours suit being served over green beans — cooked before the curry and reheated in boiling water just before serving. Add rice, too, for big eaters.

SALMON AND TOMATO CURRY SERVES 4

PREP: 20 MINUTES
COOK: 25 MINUTES

- *400g fine green beans*
- *salt and freshly ground black pepper*
- *500g vine tomatoes or 400g tin of chopped tomatoes*
- *1 teaspoon cumin seeds*
- *½ teaspoon brown or black mustard seeds*
- *1 tablespoon vegetable oil*
- *1 teaspoon dried crushed chillies*
- *2 teaspoons tamarind paste*
- *1 teaspoon ground turmeric*
- *400g tin of coconut milk*
- *a generous pinch of sugar*
- *4 x 200g fillets of salmon*
- *25g fresh coriander*

Boil a full kettle. Top and tail the beans, then cook them in salted water from the kettle in a spacious sauté or frying pan for 2 minutes. Drain the water over the fresh tomatoes (if you're using them) in a bowl, count to 30 while you refresh the beans in cold water and drain them again. Drain the tomatoes, cut out the cores in a pointed plug shape then peel and quarter them. Scrape away the seeds and chop the flesh. If you're using tinned tomatoes, sieve and rinse them to discard the seeds.

Fill and boil the kettle again. Heat the pan and quickly dry-fry the cumin and mustard seeds. Crush them lightly with the back of a wooden spoon, then add the oil, chillies, tamarind paste and turmeric, and stir-fry for a further 30 seconds before adding the coconut milk, half a teaspoon of salt and the sugar. Simmer gently for 10 minutes, then taste and adjust the seasoning with salt and sugar.

Slice the salmon into chunks. Reheat the sauce and stir in the diced tomato, heat through and add the salmon. Cook gently for 4 to 6 minutes until it is just done. While the salmon cooks, pour boiling water over the beans and leave them to heat through. Coarsely chop the coriander leaves and stir through the curry. Serve it over the beans.

The inspiration for this gentle curry came from a casual conversation with a friend. She loves food but doesn't spend a lot of time cooking and was telling me about a dish she'd bought from one of those delis that does smart ready-meals. Big pieces of chicken and plump, juicy apricots, she said, came in a bit of a sauce flavoured with saffron and large pale seeds, which might have been cardamom. A few days later I realized I'd subconsciously bought everything I needed for the dish and, bingo, here it is. I serve it with coriander-laced saffron and almond couscous, but rice would be good, or hot chapattis, lime chutney and yoghurt.

SAFFRON CHICKEN WITH APRICOTS AND CARDAMOM

SERVES 4

PREP: 20 MINUTES
COOK: 30 MINUTES

- *250g stoned traditional dried apricots*
- *a very generous pinch of saffron stamens*
- *6 cardamom pods*
- *1 tablespoon honey*
- *the juice of 4 oranges (300ml)*
- *1 large onion (250g)*
- *2 tablespoons olive oil*
- *salt and freshly ground black pepper*
- *12 boned and skinned chicken thigh fillets*
- *½ chicken stock cube*
- *a squeeze of lemon juice*
- *a few sprigs of coriander*

for the couscous:
- *½ chicken stock cube*
- *a pinch of saffron stamens*
- *1 tablespoon lemon juice*
- *1 tablespoon olive oil*
- *250g couscous*
- *10g coriander*
- *2 tablespoons toasted Marcona almonds*

Place the apricots in a large, lidded sauté or wide-based pan with the saffron, the lightly crushed cardamom pods, the honey and orange juice. Simmer gently, stirring until the honey dissolves, then cook, covered, for 20 minutes. Tip into a bowl.

While the apricots cook, peel, halve and finely slice the onion. Heat the oil in the pan and stir in the onion. Season with half a teaspoon of salt, stir again, reduce the heat to very low, cover and cook for 15 minutes, until the onion is slippery soft but hardly coloured. Move it aside and add the chicken, searing it all over for 5 minutes each side.

Dissolve the stock cube in 400ml of boiling water. Add the apricots and stock to the pan, stir well then simmer, uncovered, for 10 minutes. Taste and adjust the seasoning with salt, freshly ground black pepper and lemon juice. This dish reheats perfectly, the apricot juices thickening the sauce. Serve with the sprigs of coriander and the coriander couscous.

To make the couscous, boil a full kettle and dissolve the stock cube in 400ml of boiling water. Stir in the saffron and leave for a couple of minutes to soften. Then whisk in the lemon juice and olive oil. Place the couscous in a bowl, stir in the stock, cover and leave for 10 to 15 minutes to hydrate. Chop the coriander. Fork up the couscous, then mix in the almonds and coriander.

This is a *faux* Thai curry made without special paste but relying on fish sauce, dried crushed chillies, plenty of ginger, masses of coriander and garlic to give a recognizable Thai flavour without excessive heat. Once the sauce is made, and it's done in minutes, the cooking is quick and easy. It's a soupy dish with the vibrant crunch of mangetout and beansprouts so is good over rice noodles, any pre-soaked egg noodles or rice. Instead of chicken, it could be made with salmon, in which case slice the fillets into big chunks and avoid overcooking.

THAI TOMATO CHICKEN CURRY
WITH NOODLES SERVES 4

PREP: 20 MINUTES
COOK: 30 MINUTES

- 25g ginger
- 4 cloves of garlic
- 400g tin of chopped tomatoes
- ¼ teaspoon dried crushed chillies
- 50g bunch of coriander
- ½ tablespoon vegetable oil
- 400ml chicken stock
- 2 tablespoons Thai fish sauce
- 165ml tin coconut milk or cream
- 3 limes
- salt
- 750g chicken thigh fillets
- 150g mangetout
- 225g pre-soaked vermicelli rice noodles
- 150g beansprouts

Peel and coarsely chop the ginger and garlic. Blitz with the tomatoes, crushed chillies, stalks, roots and half the leaves of the coriander, to make a dark red speckled sauce. Heat the oil in a spacious frying or sauté pan and stir in the sauce. Cook, stirring often, over a medium heat, for 5 minutes. Add the stock, fish sauce, coconut milk or cream, the juice of 1 lime and salt to taste. Simmer for 5 minutes.

While the sauce cooks, slice the chicken into bite-size pieces. Add to the pan and simmer for a further 10 minutes. Top and tail the mangetout and halve them lengthways on the diagonal. Five minutes before you are ready to serve, soak the noodles in boiling water. Check the seasoning of the curry, then add the mangetout and, 2 minutes later, the beansprouts. Cook for 2 more minutes while you chop the remaining coriander.

Drain the noodles and put them into bowls. Stir the coriander into the curry and serve with lime wedges over the warmed noodles.

for the Sri Lankan curry powder:

- 5 teaspoons coriander seeds
- 5 teaspoons cumin seeds
- 5g cinnamon bark
- 1 cardamom pod
- 2 cloves
- 1 teaspoon raw rice
- 10 curry leaves
- 10cm rampa or pandan leaf (from Thai shops)

for the curry:

- 1kg chicken thigh fillets
- 5–6 teaspoons Sri Lankan curry powder
- 2 teaspoons chilli powder (or more, if you like it really hot)
- 1 teaspoon salt
- 1 large red onion or 6 shallots
- 2 cloves of garlic
- 30g ginger
- 3 green chillies
- 2–3 tablespoons vegetable oil
- 6 curry leaves
- ¼ teaspoon saffron stamens
- ½ teaspoon fennel seeds
- ¼ teaspoon ground cinnamon
- 20ml white wine vinegar
- 1 tablespoon tamarind paste
- 300ml coconut milk
- 10cm rampa or pandan leaf
- 4 sweet potatoes (600g)
- 12 x 15g pieces of frozen organic spinach
- yoghurt
- 2 limes

Most of my friends are keen cooks and this beguiling curry recipe was passed on by my friend Suzie Marwood, who adapted it 'from a funny little book I bought at Colombo airport. It's full of things like *Kurakkan Pitto* and *Thumba Karavila* and *Fish Smore* by Manel Ratnatunga'. It requires a bit of specialized shopping for the authentic Sri Lankan curry powder but is worth the effort. My contribution of sweet potato and spinach turns the curry into a one-pot wonder. For the best flavour, make it 24 hours before you eat it.

SRI LANKAN CHICKEN CURRY WITH SWEET POTATO AND SPINACH SERVES 6

First make the curry powder. Grind all the ingredients to a powder. You need half the quantity for this recipe; the rest will keep well in an airtight container. Slice the chicken down the fillets into double-bite-size strips and place in a mixing bowl. Rub them with curry powder, chilli powder and salt. Leave them while you peel, halve and chop the onions or shallots. Peel and chop the garlic and ginger. Deseed the chillies, if you wish, then chop them.

Heat the oil in a spacious lidded sauté or frying pan or flameproof casserole, add the onion or shallots and cook over a medium heat, stirring often, until they begin to wilt, at least 15 minutes. Then add the chillies, garlic and ginger, and cook for another 5 minutes. Turn the heat up a bit and add the curry leaves, saffron, fennel seeds, cinnamon and chicken. Stir until the chicken is sealed, then add the vinegar, tamarind and about 100 ml of water. Establish a gentle simmer, then cover and cook for about 10 minutes. Add the coconut milk, *rampa* or *pandan* leaf, knotted, stir well, cover again and simmer for 20 minutes.

Meanwhile, peel the sweet potatoes and cut them into big chunks. Stir them into the pan and add the frozen spinach. Cover and cook for a further 20 minutes. Swirl the spinach to loosen it, and serve with a bowl of yoghurt and lime wedges to squeeze over the top.

for the curry paste:

- *20 dried red chillies, 10cm long*
- *10 red bird's eye chillies*
- *125g Thai pink shallots*
- *1 tablespoon coriander seeds*
- *1 scant tablespoon cumin seeds*
- *3–4 lemongrass stalks*
- *1 tbsp chopped coriander root*
- *1 teaspoon white pepper*

for the curry:

- *300ml coconut cream*
- *250ml chicken stock*
- *4 tablespoons curry paste*
- *½ tablespoon turmeric*
- *1 teaspoon toasted ground coriander seeds*
- *½ teaspoon toasted ground cumin seeds*
- *a generous grating of nutmeg*
- *6 jointed duck legs*
- *750g medium-size waxy potatoes*
- *12 Thai pink shallots*
- *1 pandan leaf*
- *2cm piece cassia or cinnamon*
- *½–1 tablespoon palm sugar or maple syrup*
- *2–4 tablespoons Thai fish sauce*
- *400ml coconut milk*
- *50g bunch of coriander*

for the cucumber relish:

- *3 tablespoons white wine vinegar*
- *2 tablespoons white sugar*
- *1 Lebanese cucumber*
- *4 Thai pink shallots*
- *2 tablespoons julienned ginger*
- *2 tablespoon chopped coriander*
- *1 finely sliced red chilli*

I watched spellbound as David Thompson, chef of Nahm in Bangkok (www.david-thompsonthaifood.com), demonstrated for three hours at the first Ballymaloe Literary Festival of Food in May 2013 and I hope he will forgive my version of his Massaman-like curry, which is modified slightly for convenience.

THAI DUCK AND POTATO CURRY WITH CUCUMBER RELISH SERVES 4

For the curry paste, remove the seeds from the dried chillies. Stir-fry the bird's eye chillies until charred in a heavy-bottomed frying pan. Repeat with the unpeeled shallots, continuing until the flesh is yielding. Cool, peel and chop the chillies and the shallots. Stir-fry the coriander and cumin seeds in the pan. Peel away the hard outer layers of the lemongrass and finely chop the tender inner stems. Pound it (or blitz with 4 tablespoons of water) with a generous pinch of salt, then add all the other ingredients (one at a time if pounding, all together if blitzing) to make a fine paste of indistinguishable ingredients.

Heat the coconut cream with the paste in a spacious pan that can hold all the ingredients, stirring in the turmeric, coriander, cumin and nutmeg. Simmer for a few minutes to consolidate, not worrying if the oil separates from the coconut cream, then add the duck and half the stock. Simmer gently, stirring often, for about 40 minutes until the duck is very tender.

Scrub or scrape the potatoes, halve lengthways, rinse and add to the pan with the peeled shallots, knotted *pandan* leaf and cassia or cinnamon bark. Taste and season the curry with sugar or maple syrup and fish sauce, salt and freshly ground white pepper. Pour in the coconut milk and remaining stock, and simmer for about 20 minutes until the potatoes and shallots are tender. Finely chop the coriander and stir into the curry.

To make the cucumber relish, combine the vinegar, sugar, 4 tablespoons water and a pinch of salt in a small saucepan and bring to the boil. Swirl as the sugar dissolves, then cool. Quarter the cucumber lengthways, hold the pieces together and slice across to make tiny scraps. Peel and finely slice the shallots. Mix the prepared ingredients with the ginger, coriander and chilli in a serving bowl, pour over the liquid and serve.

Pasta

ARTICHOKE LINGUINE WITH
GREEN OLIVES AND PARMESAN

ROCKET AND FETA PASTA
WITH FRESH TOMATO SAUCE

RED ORZO RISOTTO
WITH GOAT'S CHEESE

BLACK PASTA WITH GARLIC
OLIVE OIL AND CHILLI

SPINACH TAGLIATELLE WITH ASPARAGUS,
GOAT'S CHEESE AND SAN DANIELE

SPAGHETTI *ALLE VONGOLE BIANCO*

CONCHIGLIE WITH CRAB,
CHILLI AND CUCUMBER

DUCK *RAGÙ* WITH CASARECCE

FRESH SPAGHETTI WITH LEEKS,
PARMA HAM AND HAZELNUTS

FIDEUA CON ALLIOLI

Artichoke hearts in olive oil are a useful store-cupboard standby. They are a welcome addition to a mezze-style spread and delicious with cannellini beans, particularly in salads with roasted red peppers and black olives. All of those ingredients would be good stirred into hot pasta but this combination of grilled or marinated artichoke hearts with masses of grassy flat-leaf parsley, pitted green olives, a lemon and olive-oil dressing and flakes of Parmesan offers a terrific variety of texture and flavour. It adapts easily for fewer or more servings.

ARTICHOKE LINGUINE WITH GREEN OLIVES AND PARMESAN SERVES 4

PREP: 15 MINUTES
COOK: 15 MINUTES

- *400g linguine*
- *salt and freshly ground black pepper*
- *2 x 260g jars grilled artichoke hearts*
- *50g flat-leaf parsley*
- *75g large pitted green olives*
- *2 large lemons*
- *6–8 tablespoons your best olive oil*
- *40g piece of Parmesan*

Boil the kettle. Use the water to cook the linguine until *al dente* with a teaspoon of salt. Meanwhile, halve the artichokes, if necessary, to make bite-size pieces. Finely chop the parsley leaves. Cut the olives into thirds. When the pasta is cooked, drain it and return it to the pan. Add the artichokes, parsley, olives and the juice from 1½ lemons. Stir in 6 tablespoons of olive oil. Season lightly with salt and generously with freshly ground black pepper.

Taste, and fine-tune the flavours with more lemon juice and/or olive oil if you think it needs it. Use a potato peeler to shave flakes of Parmesan over the top. Toss again and serve. This is good eaten with garlic bread.

If you are a gardener you will know that rocket grows like a weed. It runs rampant over my allotment, and during the summer I'm always dreaming up ways to use it. I've put handfuls into pesto instead of basil and repeatedly made a Tuscan peasant soup with rocket, stale bread and potatoes, plus countless salads, but I'm addicted to it with pasta.

For this recipe, you can use any pasta, but the short, stumpy varieties will hold the chopped rocket particularly well. Its peppery flavour is echoed by the crushed garlic and softened with a generous crumble of creamy, tangy feta cheese and olive oil, the flavours pointed up with a squeeze of lemon. This simple combination looks stunning and tastes unbelievably delicious with a dollop of fresh tomato sauce.

ROCKET AND FETA PASTA WITH
FRESH TOMATO SAUCE SERVES 4

PREP: 20 MINUTES
COOK: 30 MINUTES

- *400g penne, fusilli or other stumpy pasta*
- *a large bunch of wild rocket, minimum 110g*
- *2 cloves of garlic*
- *4 tablespoons fruity olive oil, preferably Greek, plus an extra splash*
- *½ large lemon*
- *200g Greek feta cheese*

for the tomato sauce:
- *6 large vine tomatoes, approx. 750g*
- *2 cloves of garlic*
- *a pinch of Maldon sea salt*
- *1 tablespoon olive oil*
- *freshly ground black pepper*

Begin with the tomato sauce. Place the tomatoes in a bowl, cover them with boiling water, count to 30 and drain, then cut out the cores in a pointed plug shape. Peel, quarter and chop the tomatoes. Peel and crush the garlic with a pinch of Maldon sea salt. Place the tomatoes, garlic and olive oil in a spacious pan - later it will be used for cooking the pasta. Season with black pepper and cook briskly, stirring often, for 15 to 20 minutes, until thick. For a smooth finish, pass the sauce through a sieve. Leave it to cool.

Cook the pasta according to the packet instructions. Drain and return it to the pan. While it cooks, finely chop the rocket, stalks and all. Peel the garlic, then crush it to a paste. Stir the rocket through the pasta. Add the garlic, olive oil and lemon juice and toss well. Crumble the feta over the top and stir again. Serve with a dollop of cold tomato sauce and a final swirl of olive oil.

Orzo is sometimes called the soup pasta because its shape and size, like grains of rice, are perfect for minestrone-type soups. It's great, too, for *faux* risotto, saving time and effort, yet behaving beautifully and giving a silky mouthful with a creamy finish. It takes about 10 minutes to cook in boiling, salted water, almost the amount of time you need to make a chunky red pepper, red onion and tomato *sofrito*. It is cooked in olive oil and flavoured with saffron, garlic and flat-leaf parsley. It could be made with freshly roasted peppers, preferably the long, pointed Romano variety that cooks very quickly, or you could cheat, as I did, and use roasted *piquillo* peppers in a jar. The finest, from Spain, are bottled in olive oil but the Fragata brand, using *piquillos* from Peru, is a fraction of the cost.

RED ORZO RISOTTO WITH GOAT'S CHEESE SERVES 3–4

PREP: 15 MINUTES
COOK: 20 MINUTES

• *250g orzo pasta*
• *salt*
• *2 tablespoons olive oil*
• *1 red onion*
• *1 large clove of garlic*
• *150g roasted or chargrilled Romano or piquillo peppers*
• *a pinch of saffron stamens*
• *4 vine tomatoes (200g)*
• *70g pitted dry black olives (a Crespo sachet)*
• *10g flat-leaf parsley leaves*
• *100g soft goat's cheese (Coeur de Lion, Chavroux)*

Cook the orzo in plenty of boiling salted water in a spacious, lidded sauté or frying pan, stirring once to prevent sticking, for about 10 minutes until just tender. Drain, but reserve a mugful of the cooking water. Tip the pasta into a warmed bowl, toss with 1 tablespoon of the olive oil and 2 tablespoons of the cooking water, then cover with a stretch of clingfilm.

Trim, halve and slice the onion. Heat the other tablespoon of olive oil in the pan and add in the onion. Cook, stirring often, for 6 or 7 minutes. Peel the garlic and crush it to a paste with a pinch of salt. Peel the roasted Romano peppers, if using. Slice them or the *piquillos* into ribbons and chop a few times. Stir the garlic into the onion, add 2 tablespoons of the orzo cooking water, cover, reduce the heat and cook for 10 minutes. Add the saffron and mix it in, followed by the peppers.

Quarter the tomatoes and blitz them into passata. Pour it into the pan. Simmer for a few minutes until juicy but not too wet. Mix in the drained pasta and turn off the heat. Halve the olives round their middles and chop the parsley leaves. Stir both into the pasta. Serve with a few teaspoons of goat's cheese.

This stunning recipe is based on *spaghetti aglio olio peperoncino*. Using cuttlefish-ink-dyed pasta from Puglia (www.carlu-ccios.com) gives the dish an extra dimension of flavour but it's the look that is so dramatic. The simplicity of the dish belies the flavour but pasta speckled with chilli fried in quite a lot of olive oil is powerful. I like it with a few flecks of flat-leaf parsley but that's an optional extra. It certainly helps to solve garlicky breath.

Unless you are a chilli addict, I'd recommend using the milder, longer red chillies instead of bird's eye. They lose some of their heat in the cooking but it's an eye-watering dish anyway. Traditionally it is made with spaghettini but spaghetti is good too.

BLACK PASTA WITH GARLIC OLIVE OIL AND CHILLI SERVES 2

PREP: 10 MINUTES
COOK: 15 MINUTES

- *200g pasta with cuttlefish ink (spaghetti al nero di sepia)*
- *salt*
- *6 tablespoons your best olive oil*
- *3 cloves of garlic*
- *2 mild red chillies, 12cm long*

Boil a full kettle. Pour the water into a spacious pan, return it to the boil, add a teaspoon of salt and the pasta. Cook until it is *al dente*. Drain it in a colander, tip it into a warmed bowl and toss it with a tablespoon of the olive oil. Cover with a stretch of clingfilm.

While the pasta cooks, peel the garlic, leaving it whole. Halve the chillies lengthways, scrape out the seeds and slice thinly on the diagonal. Heat the remaining oil in the pasta pan. Add the garlic and cook until it is golden, then discard it. Put in the chilli and stir-fry until it wilts. Off the heat, scoop the chilli out of the pan. Return the pasta and toss thoroughly to coat with oil, add the chilli and toss again. Serve from the pan or return it to the warm bowl, but make sure the plates are very hot. Don't delay: devour.

Look out for olive green spelt tagliatelle flavoured with spinach for this light, simple and utterly delicious pasta dish. The tagliatelle comes in short lengths, like semi-circles, and cooks quickly. It can be kept waiting for a couple of minutes while the asparagus cooks in the same water and the ham is fried quickly in olive oil. Everything comes together with chunks of soft goat's cheese, which melt against the hot food, anointing the pasta with an almost-sauce.

If you can't track down spinach tagliatelle (www.biona. co.uk), use short pasta, like tacconelli or cavatelli, rather than regular tagliatelle, which tends to be long and wide. It's too unwieldy with these ingredients.

SPINACH TAGLIATELLE WITH ASPARAGUS, GOAT'S CHEESE AND SAN DANIELE SERVES 4

PREP: 15 MINUTES
COOK: 15 MINUTES

• *250g spinach-flavoured spelt tagliatelle*

• *salt*

• *2 tablespoons olive oil*

• *400g British asparagus tips*

• *7-slice packet of San Daniele or other prosciutto*

• *2 x Soignon or other goat's cheese logs, 125g each*

Bring a large pan of water to the boil. Add a teaspoon of salt and the pasta. Boil for 4 to 5 minutes until it is *al dente*. Scoop it out of the pan into a warmed serving bowl. Stir in a tablespoon of the olive oil and cover with a stretch of clingfilm.

While the pasta cooks, cut off the tips of the asparagus and slice the stalks into similar-length pieces. Slice the ham into strips and break apart the pieces. Cut the skin, or hard bloom, off the cheese and chop the rest into sugar-lump-size pieces.

Drop the asparagus into the boiling pasta water and cook for 2 minutes. Drain and add it to the pasta, then cover the bowl again. Put the remaining oil into the pan and fry the ham until it shrivels slightly. Add it to the pasta and toss. Throw in the cheese, toss again and serve.

Fresh is always best but many fishmongers keeps bags of small clams in the deep freeze. They can also be bought online and delivered frozen (www.thefishsociety.co.uk). Once the clams have been scrubbed, rinsed and drained, the shallots, garlic and parsley chopped, the dish takes moments to cook. It's one of those one-pot three stagers: first pasta, then sauce, then the two together. Have crusty bread and butter on hand to soak up the gorgeous juices, and a bottle of chilled white wine. This is also good, incidentally, with a peeled, seeded and diced tomato added with the parsley. It then becomes *spaghetti alle vongole*.

SPAGHETTI *ALLE VONGOLE BIANCO* SERVES 4

PREP: 15 MINUTES
COOK: 15 MINUTES

• *750g small clams*
• *300g spaghetti or spaghettini*
• *salt*
• *½ small red chilli, optional*
• *2 shallots*
• *2 cloves of garlic*
• *25g flat-leaf parsley*
• *4 tablespoons olive oil*
• *150ml dry white wine*

Scrub the clams with a nail-brush, then rinse in a couple of changes of water until the water remains clear. Discard any clams with cracked shells. Cook the spaghetti in plenty of boiling salted water in a wide-based pan until it is *al dente*. Drain, then tip it into a warmed bowl and cover with a stretch of clingfilm.

Finely chop the chilli, discarding the seeds. Peel and finely chop the shallots. Peel the garlic and slice it into thin rounds. Pick the leaves off the parsley stalks and chop the leaves. Heat half of the olive oil in the pan and gently soften the shallots, chilli and garlic for 3 to 4 minutes until soft but not coloured. Add the wine, simmer to reduce by half, then put in the clams. Cook briskly for 2 to 3 minutes until all the clams are open, discarding any that remain closed. Add the spaghetti and parsley, toss together and pour over the last of the olive oil. Serve immediately.

I love fresh crab and here's a great way of turning a couple of those little pots of freshly picked Cornish crab (www. seafoodandeatit.co.uk for stockists) into a classy pasta supper. Conchiglie is the shell pasta and some of the crab ends up trapped inside the curls, giving occasional mouthfuls an extra lusciousness. The crab is mixed with plenty of finely chopped chilli, its harshness softened with olive oil and deflected by juicy peeled cucumber moons and lemon juice, with the tang of flat-leaf parsley. It's a harmonious combination that is also good spooned into crisp lettuce or piled onto hot toast, or over peeled broad beans, although it goes further stirred into pasta.

This is a huge amount for two but this salad supper is incredibly moreish so expect to eat plenty. Leftovers are good cold, a real treat for the lunch box (if it can be stashed in the fridge at work during the morning) but don't forget to pack a fork.

CONCHIGLIE WITH CRAB, CHILLI AND CUCUMBER SERVES 4

PREP: 15 MINUTES
COOK: 15 MINUTES

- *300g conchiglie pasta*
- *salt and freshly ground black pepper*
- *2 red bird's eye chillies*
- *3 tablespoons your best olive oil*
- *1 Lebanese cucumber or 10cm regular cucumber*
- *1 small lemon*
- *50g flat-leaf parsley*
- *100g freshly picked white crab meat*
- *100g freshly picked brown crab meat*

Cook the pasta in plenty of salted boiling water, according to the packet instructions — mine took 13 minutes, which is almost the perfect amount of time to make the sauce.

Trim, split and scrape the seeds from the chillies. Slice them into strips, then tiny dice. Place them in a cup with the olive oil. Use a potato peeler to peel the cucumber. Split it in half and use a teaspoon to scrape out the seeds, then slice it into 2mm-thick half-moons and put it into a bowl. Add a generous pinch of salt and the juice from the lemon. Toss it a few times as the cucumber wilts. Drain the pasta and return it to the pan. Add the cucumber and its juices and toss. Leave it for a couple of minutes while you pick the leaves off the parsley stalks and finely chop them.

Mix the crab, the chilli oil and parsley together. Stir it into the pasta. Tip into a warmed serving bowl, toss again with a pinch of sea salt and freshly grated black pepper Bingo, it's ready.

I used tender, quick-cooking Gressingham duck breast for this pasta sauce, which ends up thick and luscious, dark and aromatic, the duck hardly distinguishable from the onion, carrot and celery it's cooked with. Dried mushrooms, preferably Italian *porcini*, give the sauce a woodland back-taste complemented by tomato, fresh thyme and sage. Red wine and chicken stock bubble with the other ingredients and fill the house with mouth-watering aromas, until the sauce is ready to be mixed with *al dente* pasta and freshly grated Parmesan. It reheats perfectly.

DUCK *RAGÙ* WITH CASARECCE   SERVES 4

PREP: 20 MINUTES
COOK: 45 MINUTES

• *15g dried porcini or wild mushrooms*

• *1 medium onion*

• *1 clove of garlic*

• *1½ tablespoons olive oil*

• *1 stick of celery*

• *2 carrots (175g)*

• *a few sprigs of fresh thyme*

• *2 sage leaves*

• *salt and freshly ground black pepper*

• *a pinch of dried crushed chillies*

• *2 Gressingham duck breast fillets*

• *3–4 vine tomatoes (300g)*

• *200ml red wine*

• *250ml chicken stock*

• *400g casarecci, fusilli, penne or large macaroni*

• *Parmesan, to serve*

Place the mushrooms in a bowl, cover them with warm water and leave them to hydrate while you peel and finely chop the onion and garlic. Warm the oil in a heavy-based, lidded pan that can hold all the ingredients over a medium-low heat. Trim and finely chop the celery (peeled first if it's very fibrous). Scrape and finely dice the carrot. Strip the leaves from the sprigs of thyme, then finely chop the thyme and sage leaves. Stir all of these ingredients into the onions, add a generous pinch of salt, some freshly ground black pepper and the crushed chillies. Cover and sweat the vegetables and herbs, stirring occasionally, while you slice the duck off its skin. Chop the flesh into tiny dice; do this by hand or use a mincer.

Halve, then blitz the tomatoes into passata. Finely chop the mushrooms. Stir them, then the duck into the softening vegetables to brown. Add the wine and let it bubble, followed by the passata and the stock. Adjust the heat, semi-cover the pan and leave to simmer, stirring occasionally, for 30 minutes. Remove the lid, increase the heat slightly and simmer until the sauce is thick and creamy. Taste and adjust the seasoning, then tip it into a bowl. Wash the pan and cook the pasta until it is *al dente*. Drain the pasta, return it to the pan, stir in the sauce, heat through and serve.

I was tipped off about this simple but extraordinarily good way of cooking prosciutto with leeks and pasta by the Consorzio del Prosciutto de Parma during a special lunch at the Connaught Hotel in London to show off the versatility of Parma ham. Roasting or frying those soft, slippery sheets of rosy ham intensifies the flavour: perfect for this simple dish of shredded ham and leeks cooked in butter, then mixed with thin egg pasta. Crushed hazelnuts and a splash of syrupy balsamic vinegar make the dish classy enough to serve as a dinner-party starter, but it's so moreish, easy to make and shop for, that it's a regular TV dinner Chez Lindsey.

FRESH SPAGHETTI WITH LEEKS, PARMA HAM AND HAZELNUTS SERVES 4

PREP: 15 MINUTES
COOK: 10 MINUTES

- *2 trimmed leeks (300g)*
- *7 slices of Parma ham*
- *100g butter*
- *500g fresh egg spaghetti or other fine egg pasta*
- *salt*
- *1 tablespoon syrupy balsamic vinegar, such as Belazu*
- *50g chopped toasted hazelnuts*

Fill and boil the kettle. Cut the leeks into 8cm lengths. Split them lengthways, then slice finely into julienne. Make a pile of the ham and slice across the depth to make similar size strips. Melt the butter in a spacious wide-based pan and toss in the ham, then cook over a low heat for a couple of minutes.

Add the leeks and continue to cook, stirring occasionally, for about 8 minutes until the leeks are soft and the ham beginning to crisp. Scoop everything out of the pan into a warmed bowl and cover with a stretch of clingfilm.

Using the kettle water, boil the spaghetti with a teaspoon of salt for 2 minutes. Drain and return it to the pan. Stir in the buttery leeks and ham. Serve with a dribble of balsamic vinegar, the chopped hazelnuts scattered over the top.

Fideua are the thin, short lengths of vermicelli-like pasta used instead of rice for seafood paella. Both the pasta and this style of paella are little known outside Valencia but deserve wider recognition not least because they cook far faster than paella. This dish reminds me of an elegant, no-fuss spaghetti marinara.

FIDEUA CON ALLIOLI SERVES 6

PREP: 30 MINUTES
COOK: 20 MINUTES

- *You will need:* a 34cm paella pan
- *400g raw whole prawns*
- *400g monkfish tail*
- *salt*
- *32 mussels*
- *1 kg small cleaned squid with tentacles*
- *6 vine tomatoes (750g)*
- *6 roasted piquillo peppers, from a jar*
- *2 cloves of garlic*
- *3 tablespoons olive oil*
- *a generous pinch of saffron stamens*
- *1 teaspoon paprika*
- *600g vermicelli or other very fine noodles*
- *lemon wedges, to serve*

for the allioli:

- *2 cloves of garlic*
- *2 large egg yolks, at room temperature*
- *1 rounded teaspoon Dijon mustard*
- *250ml groundnut oil*
- *50ml light extra-virgin olive oil*
- *1–2 tablespoons lemon juice*
- *1 tablespoon warm water*
- *salt*

Peel the prawns and put the heads and shells into a pan with 2 litres of water. Slice the monkfish off the bone and add that to the pan with a pinch of salt. Simmer for 20 minutes. Strain into a jug or bowl. Scrub the mussels and rinse them in several changes of cold water. Pull off the 'beards', scrape away any barnacles and discard all broken or open mussels that don't close after a sharp tap. Drain in a colander.

Slice the squid into strips or rings. Put the tomatoes into a bowl, cover them with boiling water and count to 30. Drain, peel and quarter them. Discard the seeds and core and chop the flesh. Slice the peppers into strips. Peel the garlic, chop it, then crush it to a paste with a pinch of salt.

Heat the olive oil in the paella pan and quickly sauté the seafood to seal the squid and monkfish and turn the prawns pink. Scoop them out of the pan. Stir in the garlic, saffron and paprika, then the tomatoes. Simmer for 10 minutes.

Stir the noodles into the tomato sauce and add 900ml of the hot fish stock. Simmer briskly for 10 to 15 minutes, then spread the seafood around the pan, adding the unopened mussels. Cook for a further 3 minutes until most of the liquid has been absorbed and the mussels are opening. Loosely cover the pan with foil and cook for 5 to 10 minutes until all the mussels have opened and the pasta is tender. This final stage can be done in the oven preheated to 180°C/gas mark 4.

To make the *allioli*, peel and chop the garlic. Whisk the egg yolks and mustard together in a food processor. Combine the 2 oils in a jug, and, with the motor running, add the oil extremely slowly in a thin stream, scraping down the sides from time to time.

When you have used about half the oil, add a tablespoon of the lemon juice. Continue trickling in the oil until the mayonnaise is thick and glossy. Add the water, salt, garlic and more lemon juice if necessary. Cover with clingfilm, letting it sag to touch the *allioli*, and chill until required. Serve the *fideua* from the pan with lemon wedges and a dollop of *allioli*.

Noodles

SEAFOOD *LAKSA*

PAD THAI

SINGAPORE NOODLES

SALMON *CONFIT*, BROWN SHRIMP
AND SAMPHIRE NOODLES

HOT AND SOUR PRAWN NOODLES

BEEF *CHAP CHAE*

ASIAN NOODLES WITH
CHICKEN AND LIME

CHINESE BELLY PORK NOODLES

POMEGRANATE AND GINGER
LAMB NOODLES

VIETNAMESE *BO PHO*

A Singaporean friend introduced me to *laksa* and it was years before I had the confidence to make this seafood noodle soup with its addictively sweet, sour, hot and spicy coconut broth. It's a bit like making a Thai curry so recipes vary. Mine is flavoured with lemongrass, galangal, coriander seeds, chilli, fermented shrimp paste, called *blachan*, and shallots, with turmeric for colour and macadamia nuts to thicken the soup. I prefer tagliatelle-style rice noodles but it is often made with a thin vermicelli type. This *laksa* is a mix of prawns and baby squid with bamboo shoots as well as beansprouts for crunch and lime to sharpen the flavours.

SEAFOOD *LAKSA* SERVES 4

Crack the lemongrass with something heavy, peel away the outer layers and finely chop the tender inner shoot. Peel and chop the galangal and onion. Place them in the bowl of a food processor with the dried crushed chillies, coriander seeds, fish sauce, sugar, fermented shrimp paste, turmeric, nuts, oil, the juice of 1 lime and 2 tablespoons of the coconut milk. Blitz until the mixture is smooth. Tip it into a spacious sauté pan and cook, stirring constantly, over a low heat for 5 minutes. Add the rest of the coconut milk and the fish stock. Simmer, stirring often, for 15 minutes. Drain the bamboo shoots. Rinse the beansprouts. Peel, trim and finely slice the spring onions. Finely chop the coriander. Soak the noodles in boiling water for 10 to 15 minutes until soft.

Remove the tentacles from inside the squid sac. Quarter the sac lengthways. Stir the bamboo shoots into the simmering sauce, taste and adjust the seasoning with salt and lime juice. When it is simmering gently, add all the squid and, a couple of minutes later when it's firm and curled, drop in the prawns. The soup is ready when the prawns are pink. Serve immediately or gently reheat later.

To serve, place a mound of drained noodles in deep, wide soup bowls, top with a handful of beansprouts, the onions, then spoon over the *laksa*. Scatter over the coriander and put a lime wedge on top.

PREP: 35 MINUTES
COOK: 40 MINUTES

- *2 lemongrass stalks*
- *50g galangal or ginger*
- *1 large onion*
- *1 teaspoon dried crushed chillies*
- *2 teaspoons toasted coriander seeds*
- *2 tablespoons Thai fish sauce*
- *1 teaspoon sugar*
- *1 teaspoon fermented shrimp paste (blachan)*
- *1 teaspoon turmeric*
- *6 macadamia nuts*
- *½ tablespoon vegetable oil*
- *3 limes*
- *400ml tin of coconut milk*
- *400ml fish stock*
- *225g sachet or tin of bamboo shoots*
- *150g beansprouts*
- *4 spring onions*
- *25g coriander*
- *200g tagliatelle-style rice noodles (rice sticks)*
- *500g prepared squid*
- *salt*
- *400g raw peeled jumbo king prawns*

It's the final squeeze of lime, the crunch of chopped peanuts, the silky rice noodles with their tangy, eggy tamarind gravy, fresh coriander and lightly cooked prawns that make this everyone's favourite Thai noodle dish. I went through a phase of eating it once a week when there was a very good Thai restaurant (Sabai Sabai) close to where I live, but these days I have to make my own. It is very moreish, hence serves 2–4.

PAD THAI SERVES 2–4

PREP: 15 MINUTES
COOK: 15 MINUTES

• 200g tagliatelle-style rice noodles (rice sticks)

• 1 clove of garlic

• 4 pink Thai shallots or 1 shallot

• 4 spring onions

• 150g beansprouts

• 4 tablespoons toasted and salted cashews or peanuts

• 1 tablespoon vegetable oil

• 1 tablespoon Thai fish sauce

• 1 tablespoon tamarind paste

• 1 egg

• 200g raw peeled king prawns

• 2 tablespoons chopped coriander

• 2 limes

• Thai sweet chilli sauce

Soak the rice noodles in hot water for about 10 minutes while you prepare everything else. Peel and finely chop the garlic and shallots. Trim, halve and shred the spring onions lengthways. Rinse the beansprouts and shake them dry. Coarsely grind the nuts in a blender or food processor, or smash with a rolling pin in a plastic bag.

Drain the noodles; they should be semi-soft. Heat a wok over a high heat, add the oil and swirl it around before you start cooking. Add the garlic and shallots, stir-frying constantly for a few seconds. Put in the fish sauce and the tamarind paste, then the drained noodles. Toss constantly to mix and stir-fry. Move everything to the side, add the egg and scramble it with chopsticks, then mix with the noodles.

Add the prawns, tossing for a couple of minutes until they turn pink, then add the spring onions, beansprouts and coriander. Stir-fry for another minute or so. Serve topped with chopped nuts, a lime wedge and a dribble of sweet chilli sauce.

When I arrived at Singapore airport en route for Sydney, the first thing I did was search for somewhere to eat Singapore noodles. After the long flight I was craving comfort food but wanted fresh crunch too, so this hybrid of Indian and Chinese flavours was perfect. Spicy with curry paste and fresh chilli, the flavours are fresh and juicy, too, with beansprouts, slivers of red or green pepper, spring onions and ginger, the back-taste pungent with dried shrimp and scraps of hauntingly flavoured *char siu* pork. Back home I often make this with leftovers from the Sunday joint instead of seeking out Chinese barbecued pork in Chinatown. Once the dried shrimp has been soaked, it's a quick stir-fry so have all the ingredients prepared in separate piles ready to go.

SINGAPORE NOODLES SERVES 2

PREP: 15 MINUTES
COOK: 25 MINUTES

• 2 tablespoons dried shrimp

• 1 large onion

• 3 cloves of garlic

• 25g ginger

• 1 red or green pepper

• 150g beansprouts

• 125g bunch of spring onions

• 1 long red chilli

• 100g char siu pork, roasted pork or chicken

• 300g prepared rice vermicelli noodles

• 2 tablespoons vegetable oil

• 1 tablespoon hot curry paste

• 2 tablespoons Kikkoman soy sauce

• Thai fish sauce and sugar to taste

Place the dried shrimp in a bowl. Cover with boiling water and leave to soak for 20 minutes. Peel, halve and finely slice the onion. Crack the garlic, flake away the skin and finely slice it into rounds. Peel and finely slice the ginger into shirt-button size pieces. Halve the pepper, remove the seeds and white membrane, then slice thinly down the halves. Rinse the beansprouts in a colander and shake them dry. Trim and finely slice the spring onions on the diagonal in long, thin pieces. Halve the chilli round the middle. Finely slice the pointed end and finely chop the rest, discarding the seeds. Finely slice the pork or chicken. Soak the noodles in boiling water for 5 minutes. Rinse and drain them.

Heat a wok, add the oil, and stir-fry the garlic and ginger for 30 seconds. Add the onion, reduce the heat and stir-fry for about 10 minutes until succulent. Throw in the pepper and the drained shrimp, then toss.

Add the pork, curry paste, soy sauce, drained noodles and beansprouts. Toss, then pop in the spring onions and chillies, stir-frying until the spring onions are wilted. Season to taste with Thai fish sauce and sugar. Pile into bowls and enjoy.

Bruno Loubet is a chef I have admired since my early days as a restaurant critic. He is clever with vegetables and fish and I learned this way of cheating at salmon *confit* from his book *Mange Tout*, and it's a technique he uses at his latest restaurant, the Grain Store in London's King's Cross. The fish ends up silky while retaining its true deep colour and slips over noodles with samphire and little brown shrimps, everything bathed in citrus vinaigrette. To make more or fewer servings, increase or decrease all of the ingredients in proportion.

SALMON *CONFIT*, BROWN SHRIMP AND SAMPHIRE NOODLES SERVES 4

PREP: 15 MINUTES
COOK: 15 MINUTES, PLUS
30 MINUTES COOKING

- *4 x 200g skinned fillets of salmon*
- *1 tablespoon olive oil*
- *150g fresh samphire*
- *2 x 275g bags of cooked fine egg noodles*
- *150g packet of peeled brown shrimps*

for the vinaigrette:

- *1 teaspoon runny honey*
- *1 tablespoon lime juice*
- *2 tablespoons fresh orange juice*
- *3 tablespoons olive oil*

Boil the kettle. Turn the oven to 100°C/gas mark ½. Generously smear the salmon with the olive oil and place it in a small roasting tin. Roast for 15 minutes. Transfer to a plate and cover with a stretch of clingfilm. Leave to cool.

Trim the woody ends from the samphire and place it in a large bowl. Generously cover with boiling water and a stretch of clingfilm. Leave for at least 10 minutes, possibly 15, until juicy yet firm. Refill the kettle and boil it again. Place the noodles in a second bowl, then cover them with boiling water and clingfilm. Leave them to warm through.

Make the vinaigrette in a serving bowl whisking all the ingredients together. Drain the noodles and samphire and stir through the vinaigrette. Add the shrimps, flake the salmon in big pieces over the top, then toss and serve.

Pink and green, crunch and slurp: that's the theme for this noodle supper with a stingingly vibrant broth. The plump prawns, sweet bright peas and juicy celery combine to bring a fresh tang that demands your attention in this wide-awake but comforting noodle bowlful.

HOT AND SOUR PRAWN NOODLES SERVES 4

PREP: 20 MINUTES
COOK: 30 MINUTES

- *300g tagliatelle-style rice noodles*
- *300g celery heart*
- *125g bunch of spring onions*
- *1 red bird's eye chilli*
- *2 lemongrass stalks*
- *50g bunch of coriander*
- *2 kaffir lime leaves*
- *3 tablespoons Thai fish sauce*
- *2 limes*
- *1 litre boiling water*
- *½ chicken stock cube*
- *200g frozen petits pois*
- *2 x 180g raw peeled king prawns*
- *Thai sweet chilli sauce*

Place the noodles in a mixing bowl and cover with hot water from the kettle. Stir vigorously with a fork to separate the strands. Leave to soak and soften. Trim the celery, hold the stalks together and finely slice across. Rinse and shake them dry. Trim and finely slice the spring onions. Split the chilli, scrape away the seeds, slice into skinny batons and then into tiny dice. Bash the lemongrass with something heavy to crack and bruise it.

Chop the bunch of coriander working up from the stalks. Place the stalk half of the bunch with the celery, spring onions, chilli and kaffir lime leaves in a pan with 2 tablespoons of the Thai fish sauce, the juice from a lime and 1 litre boiling water. Crumble the stock cube into the pan. Stir, partially cover the pan and simmer steadily for 20 minutes. Add the peas and continue cooking uncovered until they are tender.

While that is going on, run a sharp knife down the inside length of the prawns and swipe away the black line. Taste the broth and adjust the seasoning with lime juice and fish sauce. Add the prawns. When they have all turned pink drop in the remaining coriander.

Drain the noodles and divide between 4 bowls. Pour over the broth, with the prawns and vegetables, discarding the lemongrass and lime leaves. Add a splash of chilli sauce and serve.

Chap chae, or *jap chae*, is a popular Korean noodle stir-fry with a great combination of crunch and slurp, salty and sweet, sour and spicy-hot with a hint of pickle. It makes the most of a small amount of meat and adapts perfectly with pork, chicken or lamb, all slivered like the steak in this recipe. Try it, too, with minced meat and prawns, even monkfish or squid. Ideally you want glass noodles, but wheat or rice noodles are an acceptable substitute.

BEEF *CHAP CHAE* SERVES 2–4

PREP: 20 MINUTES
COOK: 15 MINUTES

- *10g dried or 100g fresh shiitake mushrooms*
- *100g dried glass, rice or stir-fry noodles*
- *1½ tablespoons toasted sesame oil*
- *1 teaspoon toasted sesame seeds*
- *100g beef flank steak*
- *1 carrot*
- *6 spring onions*
- *1 onion (125g)*
- *25g ginger*
- *2 tablespoons Kikkoman soy sauce*
- *½ teaspoon sugar*
- *¼ teaspoon dried crushed chillies*
- *1 clove of garlic*
- *1 tablespoon vegetable oil*
- *100g young spinach*
- *1 tablespoon sweet chilli sauce, plus extra to serve*

If you're using dried shiitake, cover them with boiling water and leave for 15 minutes to hydrate. Slice in thin strips. Thinly slice fresh shiitake. Soak the noodles in boiling water for 20 minutes, then drain. Boil them for 5 minutes in a wok. Drain, rinse with cold water and toss with half a tablespoon of the sesame oil and half the sesame seeds.

Slice the steak across the grain into skinny short strips. Slice the scraped, trimmed carrot and spring onions into matchsticks. Peel, quarter and finely slice the onion. Peel the ginger, finely slice and chop it. Mix together the soy sauce, sugar, dried crushed chillies, crushed garlic and the remaining tablespoon of sesame oil.

Swirl the vegetable oil around a hot wok. Add the carrot and onion, then stir-fry for 2 minutes. Toss in the spring onions, steak, ginger and mushrooms. Continue stir-frying for a minute. Add the soy sauce mixture, the noodles, spinach and a tablespoon of sweet chilli sauce. Stir-fry until the spinach wilts. Scatter the remaining sesame seeds over the top and serve with sweet chilli sauce.

This is an addictively hot, sour and creamy Thai-style slurpy noodle meal-in-a-bowl, made with ingredients collected after a quick rush around a mini-market at closing time. Crunchy bamboo shoots, zingy coconut gravy, shredded chicken, silky egg noodles flecked with coriander, ready in no time at all. It's a make-and-eat dish: if you let it sit around, the noodles will drink up the sauce and spoil the point of the dish. It could also be made with prawns or pulled ham hock, which is sold in convenient 90g double packs.

ASIAN NOODLES WITH
CHICKEN AND LIME   SERVES 2, GENEROUSLY

PREP: 15 MINUTES
COOK: 15 MINUTES

- *6 spring onions*
- *1 unwaxed lemon*
- *10g ginger*
- *1 red bird's eye chilli*
- *3 kaffir lime leaves*
- *2 tablespoons Thai fish sauce*
- *160ml tin of coconut cream*
- *250ml chicken stock*
- *200g ready-prepared fine egg noodles*
- *150g sachet or tin of bamboo shoots*
- *25g coriander*
- *150–250g cooked chicken*
- *1 lime*

Boil the kettle. Trim and finely slice the spring onions. Remove the zest from half the lemon in paper-thin scraps. Peel and finely slice the ginger and chop it into shirt-button-size pieces. Split, deseed and finely chop the chilli. Place the spring onions, lemon zest, ginger, chilli, lime leaves and fish sauce in a pan with the coconut cream and stock. Bring to the boil, reduce the heat and simmer for 10 minutes.

Pour boiling water over the noodles and leave them for 2 minutes. Add the bamboo shoots to the coconut broth. Chop the coriander and shred the chicken. Drain the noodles and divide them between two bowls. Top them with chicken and some of the coriander. Add the remaining coriander to the broth and ladle it over the noodles. Serve with lime wedges to squeeze over the top.

Very thin slices of belly pork poached in an aromatic Chinese broth look like skinny rashers of bacon swirled over egg noodles. It's a robust bowlful with wilted bok choi, sushi ginger and coriander swirling over the noodles in the dark brown, chilli-flecked broth. Eat with chopsticks if you dare, fork and spoon if not.

CHINESE BELLY PORK NOODLES SERVES 4–6

PREP: 15 MINUTES
COOK: 90 MINUTES

- *750g–1 kg belly pork joint*
- *1 garlic bulb*
- *25g ginger*
- *2 star anise*
- *100ml sherry*
- *100ml Kikkoman soy sauce*
- *2 tablespoons balsamic vinegar*
- *½ teaspoon dried crushed chillies*
- *1 cinnamon stick*
- *2 x 275g bags of cooked egg noodles*
- *4 bok choi*
- *50g coriander*
- *25g sushi ginger*

Run a sharp cook's knife under the pork skin and its layer of fat to remove it in one piece. Place the meat in a lidded pan that can hold it snugly and cover with 750ml water. Separate the cloves of garlic and crack each one, not bothering to remove the skin. Thinly slice the unpeeled ginger. Add both to the pan with the star anise, sherry, soy sauce, balsamic vinegar, dried crushed chillies and cinnamon. Bring slowly to the boil, turn the heat very low, cover and simmer for 90 minutes.

Lift the joint onto a work surface and cover it with clingfilm until you're ready to slice it. Strain the stock and return it to a clean pan (if you're concerned about the fat content, chill it in the freezer then skim off the fat). Simmer to reduce by about a third.

Ten minutes before you're ready to serve, place the noodles in a bowl, then cover them with boiling water and a stretch of clingfilm. Quarter the bok choi lengthways and wilt it in the hot stock. Slice the pork very thinly down the length of the joint. Place the strained noodles, stock, greens, meat and some sprigs of coriander in a large bowl. Add torn slices of sushi ginger. Toss and serve. This is delicious either hot or cold. It's very good for a picnic.

A bottle of dark, exotic-smelling, tangy pomegranate syrup will last for ages even in the hands of the most adventurous cook. I use it like balsamic vinegar, the thick aged version from Belazu, which it resembles, adding a splash whenever I'm stuck for inspiration. I particularly like its haunting flavour in slowly braised lamb dishes like this one. It combines well with other powerful flavours, like soy sauce, star anise and cinnamon, in this intensely flavoured Peking-inspired sweet and sour broth. Any cut of lamb would be suitable but be sure it ends up meltingly tender so that it breaks apart with the gentle twist of a fork or chopsticks. I used shoulder and that's what I would recommend. If you're concerned about the fattiness of shoulder meat, make the dish 24 hours in advance and leave it to chill overnight for the fat to harden. It can then be scooped off and discarded. In that case, add the beans and coriander just before serving.

POMEGRANATE AND GINGER LAMB NOODLES SERVES 4

PREP: 20 MINUTES
COOK: 75 MINUTES

- 250g green beans
- salt
- 750g lamb shoulder
- 4 garlic cloves
- 2 onions
- 20g fresh ginger
- 2 tablespoons pomegranate syrup or 2 tablespoons balsamic vinegar
- 2 tablespoons soy sauce
- 2 tablespoons dry sherry
- 5cm piece of cinnamon bark
- 1 star anise
- 600ml chicken stock
- 2 tablespoons groundnut oil
- 250g medium egg noodles
- 50g coriander

Top, tail and halve the beans. Boil them in salted water for 2 minutes in a spacious, lidded pan. Drain and immerse them in cold water to arrest cooking and save the colour. Slice the lamb into strips 6 x 2cm wide. Peel the garlic and ginger and slice it into thin scraps. Peel and finely chop the onions.

Mix together the pomegranate syrup or balsamic vinegar, soy sauce, sherry, cinnamon, star anise and stock in a jug. Heat a tablespoon of the oil in the pan and quickly brown the meat in batches, transferring it to a plate as you go. Add the remaining oil and stir-fry the onion, tossing it around until it begins to wilt and colour; allow at least 15 minutes for this.

Stir in the garlic and ginger and cook for another couple of minutes. Return the meat to the pan and add the stock mixture. Slowly bring the liquid to simmering point then turn the heat very low. Cover and cook for 60 minutes or until the meat is very tender. Taste for salt. Stir in the drained beans.

Prepare the noodles according to the packet instructions – mine required a 6-minute soak. Drain and mix them with the chopped coriander. Divide the noodles between 4 deep bowls and spoon over the meat, beans and broth.

PREP: 45 MINUTES
COOK: 4 HOURS (STOCK);
30 MINUTES (SOUP)

for the stock:
- 2 large onions
- 1 whole bulb of garlic
- 2kg marrow, knuckle and/or beef shin bones
- a few chicken wings, optional
- 500g piece shin, chuck or other stewing steak, optional
- 75g fresh ginger
- 2 large carrots
- 2 star anise
- 30g rock sugar (from Chinese/ Asian stores)
- 1 cinnamon stick
- ½ teaspoon salt
- 12 black peppercorns
- 4 tablespoons Thai fish sauce

for the soup:
- 200g dried tagliatelle-style rice noodles (rice sticks)
- 250g rump, sirloin or fillet beef steak
- 300g beansprouts
- 125g bunch of spring onions
- 5 limes
- 2 long red chillies

to garnish:
- sprigs of coriander
- sprigs of Thai basil
- sprigs of mint

There is no point in attempting *pho*, the famous noodle soup of Vietnam, if you don't take trouble with the stock. It is best to make it 24 hours ahead so that the flavours mature and the fat can be thoroughly skimmed off.

The crystal-clear stock is poured over ready-prepared rice noodles, pieces of beef from the stockpot or wafer-thin slivers of fresh steak (or both) that cook in moments in the soup. A bounty of add-ons, all separately presented for diners to help themselves, include sprigs of coriander, mint and Thai basil, sliced chillies, spring onions and beansprouts. Some people include scraps of peeled tomato and finely sliced fennel or celery. *Pho* is fresh and aromatic, light and healthy and endlessly variable. My recipe is based on one served at Naga (www.nagarestaurants.co.uk) in London's Kensington.

VIETNAMESE *BO PHO* SERVES 6–8

Heat the oven to 220°C/gas mark 7. Place the unpeeled onion and garlic in a small oven dish and roast for about 25 minutes until the skin is black. Meanwhile, cover the bones with water and bring to the boil. Discard the scummy water, rinse the bones and return to the pan.

Flake away the blackened onion skin, trim the ends, break apart the garlic and place in the pan with the bones, chicken wings and stewing steak, if using, plus sliced ginger and carrots, star anise, sugar, cinnamon, salt and peppercorns. Add 4–5 litres of water to cover generously. Simmer, skimming regularly, for 4 hours. Add 3 tablespoons of the fish sauce, then more salt and fish sauce to taste. Strain. Set aside the stewing steak, if using, let it cool and wrap it in clingfilm. Cool and chill the stock overnight.

Skim off the fat. Reheat the stock. Soak the noodles in boiling water for 20 minutes, then drain. Slice the steak very thinly into bite-size sheets – 30 minutes in the freezer makes this task much easier. Rinse the beansprouts and shake them dry. Slice the spring onions. Halve the limes. Trim and slice the chillies into thin rounds. Place all of these items and the shredded stewing steak, if using, in bowls for people to help themselves.

To eat *pho*, place a mound of noodles in a deep bowl. Pour on some boiling stock, then add slivers of steak, scraps of stewing steak, if using, beansprouts, spring onions, chilli and herbs. Squeeze a half-lime over the top.

177

Noodles

Rice

SUMMER KEDGEREE
WITH LIME

COSTAS' MUSSELS

LOUISIANA JAMBALAYA

MOROCCAN LEMON AND
CHICKEN PILAFF

PAELLA BIANCO

RISI E BISI

SAFFRON ONION RICE WITH
CHICKEN AND PEAS

RISOTTO WITH SAUSAGE,
BEANS AND RED WINE

Although kedgeree is best known as a breakfast dish, the combination of rice and smoked haddock, hard-boiled eggs and curry powder works well at any time of day and year, and is a great picnic dish. Adding tomatoes might sound anarchic but they lend a welcome juiciness to what can be a dry dish. They lighten it too, giving a summery look and taste. If you don't fancy the idea, just leave them out. Kedgeree doesn't have to be eaten piping hot: it suits being served warm or cold.

SUMMER KEDGEREE WITH LIME SERVES 4

PREP: 30 MINUTES
COOK: 30 MINUTES

- 4 eggs
- 450g naturally smoked haddock
- 1 bay leaf
- 200g basmati rice
- salt
- 30g butter
- 2 onions (350g)
- 2 tablespoons vegetable oil
- 1 tablespoon curry powder or ground turmeric
- 12 vine cherry tomatoes
- 50g coriander
- 3 limes
- mango chutney

Place the eggs in a spacious lidded pan and cover with cold water. Boil for 5 minutes, then crack them all over and carefully peel under cold water. Next, place the haddock in the pan, cutting to fit, and cover with 400ml of water. Add the bay leaf, and simmer until the fish is just tender.

Lift the fish onto a plate and carefully pour the fish stock into a measuring jug, topping up, if necessary, to 300ml. Rinse the rice until the water runs clear. Put it into the pan with the fish stock and a pinch of salt. Bring to the boil, then immediately turn the heat very low, cover and cook for 10 minutes. Leave, covered, for a further 10 minutes.

Fork up the rice with 15g butter and transfer to a mixing bowl. Cover with a stretch of clingfilm. Peel, halve and finely chop the onions. Heat the oil in the clean pan, drop in the onions and cook, stirring occasionally, until they are slippery soft, golden brown and shrunken. Add 15g of the butter with the curry powder or turmeric. Stir constantly to cook the curry powder or turmeric for a couple of minutes.

Mix the rice into the onion until everything is uniformly coloured. Tip the pan contents into the mixing bowl. Flake the fish, discarding bones, over the top, adding any juices. Quarter the tomatoes and finely chop the coriander. Add both to the mixing bowl. Squeeze the juice from a lime over the top. Fold everything together, then turn onto a serving platter. Add the halved eggs and edge the dish with lime wedges. Serve with mango chutney.

Here's a great way of making a meal of mussels. It's a Greek-style pilaff and Costas is my holiday landlord in Lemnos. He makes it with the sweet mussels that grow on this fertile island, and intensely flavoured tomatoes from his garden. The salty taste of the sea that always comes from mussels is muddled through rice and tomatoes, with a hint of saffron, onions and garlic. Plenty of chopped flat-leaf parsley and more diced tomato added at the end freshen the flavours and make the dish look very pretty.

COSTAS' MUSSELS SERVES 6

PREP: 25 MINUTES
COOK: 35 MINUTES

- *2kg mussels*
- *200ml dry white wine*
- *8 vine tomatoes (750g)*
- *1 large clove of garlic, preferably new season*
- *2 onions*
- *3 tablespoons olive oil*
- *a generous pinch of saffron stamens*
- *250g long grain rice*
- *50g flat-leaf parsley*

Scrub the mussels and rinse them in several changes of cold water. Pull off the 'beards', scrape away any barnacles with the back of a small knife and discard all broken or open mussels that don't close after a sharp tap. Drain thoroughly in a colander.

Place the mussels in a large, lidded saucepan with the wine. Cover and cook at the highest possible heat, giving the pan an occasional shake to move the mussels around, for 3 to 5 minutes until all of them have opened. Drain into a colander placed over a bowl.

Measure off 750ml of the strained cooking liquid, topping up with tomato water, if necessary. To collect the tomato water, cover the tomatoes with boiling water, count to 30, drain, cut out the core in a pointed plug shape and remove the skin. Place a sieve over a bowl, quarter the tomatoes and scrape the seeds into the sieve. Crush the seeds against the sieve with the back of a spoon until the juice has run out. Chop the tomato flesh. Peel, halve and finely chop the garlic and onions.

Heat the oil in the pan and add the garlic and onions. Cook, stirring often, for about 15 minutes until soft. Add three-quarters of the chopped tomatoes and the saffron. Cook, stirring often, for 10 to 15 minutes until the tomatoes are soft and sauce-like. Stir the washed rice into the sauce, then add the liquid. Bring to the boil, reduce the heat, cover and simmer gently, for about 15 minutes until the rice is tender. Remove the cooled mussels from their shells. Stir them, with most of the chopped parsley and the remaining tomatoes, through the sloppy rice. Leave covered for 5 minutes, then scatter over the reserved parsley and serve from the pan or piled onto a warmed platter.

I ate my first jambalaya on Avery Island, where Tabasco is made, and learned to cook Louisiana's robustly spicy rice, meat and seafood stew with the help of the late Paul McIlhenny's *Tabasco Cookbook*, first published in 1993 with recipes dating back to 1868 when Edmund McIlhenny introduced Tabasco to oysters and Bloody Marys. Distantly related to paella and risotto, jambalaya is a forgiving dish, easy to make well and economical too.

LOUISIANA JAMBALAYA SERVES 4

PREP: 20 MINUTES
COOK: 50 MINUTES

- 2 onions (250g)
- 2 cloves of garlic
- 1 green or red pepper
- 1 celery heart
- 2 tablespoons vegetable oil
- 1 bay leaf
- salt and freshly ground black pepper
- ½ teaspoon cayenne pepper
- 200g raw king prawns, frozen or fresh
- ½ teaspoon Tabasco, plus extra to serve
- 3 organic chicken thigh fillets
- 250g basmati rice
- 50g sliced chorizo
- 400g tin of chopped tomatoes
- 1 chicken stock cube
- 500ml boiling water
- 25g bunch of flat-leaf parsley
- 1 lemon

Peel, halve and finely chop the onions and garlic. Halve, deseed, slice and chop the pepper into dolly-mixture-size pieces. Trim the celery, hold it together, slice it finely, then rinse and shake it dry.

Heat the oil in a spacious heavy-bottomed, lidded casserole and stir in the onions and garlic. Cook for about 5 minutes, then add the pepper, celery and bay leaf. Season with salt, freshly ground black pepper and cayenne, and cook for about 10 minutes, giving the occasional stir, while you prepare everything else.

If the prawns are frozen, slip them into a bowl of water for a few minutes to defrost, then drain. Place them or the fresh prawns in a bowl and mix with the half-teaspoon of Tabasco. Cut the chicken into bite-size pieces. Rinse the rice until the water runs clear. Stir the chicken into the vegetables and when it's changed colour, add the chorizo, rice, tomatoes and stock. Bring to a simmer, reduce the heat and stir. Cover the pan and cook for 20 minutes.

Stir in the prawns, cover and cook for a further 10 minutes or until the rice is tender. Chop the parsley leaves and stir them through the jambalaya. Serve with lemon wedges and the Tabasco bottle.

Sometimes an unexpected ingredient or two can work wonders in a familiar recipe. That's the case with this pilaff, brought to life with Moroccan salt-preserved lemons, fresh coriander, toasted pinenuts, rather than the usual almonds, and olive oil instead of ghee. The recipe comes from Sydney via my friend Tessa from her friend Jan, scribbled down years ago when we were on holiday in Greece. It's made so often in my kitchen that it feels like my recipe but thank you, Jan and Tessa.

MOROCCAN LEMON AND
CHICKEN PILAFF SERVES 4, GENEROUSLY

PREP: 15 MINUTES
COOK: 40 MINUTES

- 1 medium onion
- 2 medium carrots
- 1 stick of celery
- 3 cloves of garlic
- 4 tablespoons olive oil
- salt
- 4–5 chicken thigh fillets
- 2 Moroccan-style preserved lemons or 1 unwaxed lemon
- 75g golden sultanas
- ½ teaspoon turmeric
- 400g long grain rice
- 1 litre chicken stock or 2 chicken cubes dissolved in 1 litre boiling water
- 1 cinnamon stick
- 50g coriander
- 40g toasted pinenuts

Heat the oven to 190°C/gas mark 5. Finely chop the peeled onion, scraped carrot, trimmed, peeled celery and peeled garlic. Heat the oil in a lidded flameproof and ovenproof pan, stir in all the vegetables, season with salt, then cover and cook for 10 minutes, giving the occasional stir, or until they are tender.

Meanwhile slice the chicken into bite-size strips. Scrape the seeds and pith out of the preserved lemons and slice the skin into skinny strips. If using a fresh lemon, remove the zest in small scraps about the size of a shirt button. Stir the sliced chicken, sultanas, lemon zest and turmeric into the vegetables, then add the washed rice, stock and cinnamon stick. Bring to the boil, cover tightly and cook in the oven for 30 minutes.

Serve from the dish or transfer to a platter, with the chopped coriander and pinenuts scattered over the top.

My family is mad about paella. For one of my son's birthdays I made paella for twenty, two types, the family favourite with chorizo and squid and this new one, with chicken, fennel and mushrooms. Both went down a storm and sent wafts of complementary scents buzzing round the room but *paella bianco* — without tomato — was a gentle contrast to the lusty, strong flavours of the chorizo paella. This gentler paella is like a risotto and is finished with *gremolata*, a garlic, lemon zest and parsley sharpener, and a dollop of creamy mascarpone to melt through the rice. I made it in a huge paella pan but this scaled-down version could be cooked in a small roasting tin or spacious frying or sauté pan if you don't own a paella pan (although I urge you to get one).

PAELLA BIANCO SERVES 6, GENEROUSLY

PREP: 30 MINUTES
COOK: 40 MINUTES

- 25g dried wild mushrooms
- 2 pinches of saffron stamens
- 1 chicken stock cube
- 1 onion (125g)
- 1 tablespoon olive oil
- 2 baby fennel bulbs
- salt and freshly ground black pepper
- 6 organic chicken thigh fillets (500g)
- 200g closed-cap mushrooms
- 20 pitted green olives
- 350g bomba paella rice
- 1 unwaxed lemon
- 2 cloves of garlic
- 50g flat-leaf parsley
- 6 tablespoons mascarpone
- lemon wedges

Boil the kettle. Cover the dried mushrooms and saffron with a litre of boiling water. Crumble the stock cube over the top, give it a good stir to dissolve, and leave, covered, for 15 minutes. Peel, halve and finely chop the onion. Soften it in the olive oil in a 32cm paella pan, spacious frying or sauté pan. Cook, giving the odd stir, for 10 to 15 minutes.

Halve the fennel bulbs lengthways and thinly slice across the pieces. Add to the onions with a generous pinch of salt and black pepper. Stir occasionally while you slice the chicken into bite-size strips. Increase the heat slightly and add the chicken, turning the pieces until they are evenly coloured.

Drain the dried mushrooms, reserving the stock, and chop them coarsely. Wipe the fresh mushrooms and quarter them — halve smaller ones. Stir both into the pan, cooking for a few minutes while you halve the olives through their middles. Stir the olives then the rice through the paella.

Make the stock up to 1.2 litres with boiling water from the kettle and ladle it over the rice. Give it a good stir, to spread all the ingredients evenly, then simmer briskly. As soon as the rice starts to surface, reduce the heat and leave to simmer gently for 20 to 30 minutes until the rice has soaked up all the liquid but retains a slight bite at the centre.

Zest the lemon and peel the garlic. Chop the parsley leaves. Finely chop the zest and the garlic, then chop them again with the parsley. Scatter the mixture over the finished paella. Cover with foil and leave for 10 minutes before serving with a dollop of mascarpone and a lemon wedge.

Risi e bisi is the Venetian way of cooking new-season peas with risotto rice. It's a lovely sloppy bowlful that is neither soup nor risotto but somewhere in between and must be eaten with a spoon. I tend to think of it as a store-cupboard dish as I usually make it with frozen petits pois, which are always sweet and tender unlike fresh peas, which can be hard and dry unless very young. My version is enriched with a little pancetta or smoked streaky bacon at the start of cooking and a dollop of creamy mascarpone with grated Parmesan at the end. For extra *élan*, serve it with anchovy and Parmesan bruschetta.

RISI E BISI SERVES 3–4

PREP: 15 MINUTES
COOK: 25 MINUTES

- *3 shallots*
- *25g butter*
- *1 tablespoon olive oil*
- *75g diced pancetta or chopped smoked streaky bacon*
- *2 chicken stock cubes*
- *25g flat-leaf parsley*
- *400g podded fresh peas or frozen petits pois*
- *½ glass white wine*
- *200g arborio rice*
- *2 tablespoons mascarpone*
- *4 tablespoons grated Parmesan*

Peel, halve and finely chop the shallots. Melt the butter in the olive oil in a spacious, heavy-bottomed pan and stir in the shallots and pancetta. Cook for about 8 minutes until the shallots are soft and the pancetta or bacon is crisp. Dissolve the stock cubes in 1 litre of boiling water. Chop the flat-leaf parsley leaves.

Stir the petits pois and parsley into the shallots, then add the white wine and sufficient stock to just cover. Simmer briskly for 2 minutes, stir in the rice and add the rest of the stock. Return to the boil, immediately reduce the heat and simmer, stirring occasionally, for 15 to 20 minutes until the rice is tender. Stir in the mascarpone and a tablespoon of the grated Parmesan. Serve in bowls with a shower of Parmesan.

Easy to make and shop for, this is neither paella nor risotto but delivers the best of both: the three key ingredients — chicken, peas and onions — stand alone yet are united by the plump tender grains of rice. Onion, usually a bit-part player in paella and risotto, has a key role in this dish. Sliced quite chunkily and cooked until juicy, yet lightly burnished and stained golden by the saffron, it is almost entirely done before the other ingredients join it in the pan.

Chicken thighs, boned and sliced into chunky strips, are more suitable than breast for this dish but either fresh or frozen peas are perfect. The advantage of bomba over so-called risotto rice — arborio, carnaroli and vialone nano — is that it requires very little attention, leaving you free to go about your business. Stir basil or mint through the rice just before serving and lavish it with grated Grana Padano or Parmesan. This dish is good over green beans.

SAFFRON ONION RICE WITH CHICKEN AND PEAS SERVES 2

PREP: 15 MINUTES
COOK: 30 MINUTES

- 1 onion (150g)
- 1 tablespoon olive oil
- salt
- a generous pinch of saffron stamens
- 4 tablespoons water
- 4 chicken thigh fillets
- 1 chicken stock cube
- 600ml boiling water
- 100g fresh or frozen peas
- a handful of basil or mint leaves
- 50g chunk of Grana Padano or Parmesan
- 1 tablespoon extra virgin olive oil

Peel, halve and slice the onion into chunky half-moons. Heat the oil in a spacious sauté or frying pan and stir in the onion. Cook briskly, over a medium-high heat, for 3 to 4 minutes until it is beginning to colour and wilt. Reduce the heat slightly, add a generous pinch of salt and cook, stirring occasionally, for about 10 minutes. Add the saffron and water.

As it bubbles away, unfurl the chicken pieces and slice them across the width into chunky ribbons. Dissolve the stock cube in the boiling water. Stir the chicken into the onions and brown it thoroughly, then add the rice, peas and stock. Bring to the boil, stir, then leave to simmer steadily for 20 minutes or until the rice is plump, tender and most of the liquid has been absorbed. If, incidentally, you use risotto rice, you will need slightly less liquid. Stir in the coarsely chopped basil or mint and serve risotto-style with plenty of grated Grana Padano or Parmesan. Add a swirl of your best olive oil.

This robustly flavoured main-course risotto is inspired by *paniscia*, a speciality of Novara in Lombardy. To be authentic it should be made with stock from boiling dried pinto beans with carrots, celery and onion, enriching the flavours with a few nuggets of local pork sausage, scraps of bacon and cabbage. A tradition has grown up of cooling the dish with a splash of red wine, so when in Novara . . .

RISOTTO WITH SAUSAGE, BEANS AND RED WINE SERVES 4

PREP: 25 MINUTES
COOK: 35 MINUTES

• *1 litre chicken stock*

• *4 rashers smoked streaky bacon*

• *1 tablespoon olive oil*

• *1 onion*

• *2 sticks of celery*

• *1 decent-sized carrot*

• *300g Italian, Toulouse or other very meaty, spicy sausages*

• *1 leek*

• *salt*

• *200g carnaroli or other risotto rice*

• *a large glass of red wine*

• *25g flat-leaf parsley or basil*

• *400g tin of borlotti beans*

• *freshly grated Parmesan*

Boil the stock in a spacious, lidded frying or sauté pan, then pour it into a jug and cover to keep it hot. Slice the bacon into lardons and fry gently in the olive oil, stirring often, in the pan. Peel, halve and finely chop the onion. Dice the celery and the scraped carrot. Keep them in separate piles. Run a knife down the sausages and peel away the skin. Break them into pieces, like small uneven meatballs. Trim the leek, quarter it lengthways, hold it together and slice it into small scraps. Rinse and drain it.

Stir the onion into the bacon and cook, stirring often, for about 8 minutes until it has wilted. Stir in the celery and carrot, season with salt and toss as they begin to soften. Add the sausage and continue to toss until it is firm and nicely crusty. Throw in the leek, stirring as it wilts. Add the rice, stirring until it is glossy, then pour in the wine and let it bubble.

Tip in a quarter of the stock, stirring regularly until it has disappeared. Continue with two more lots of stock, then stir in half of the chopped parsley or basil and the drained, rinsed borlotti beans. When the risotto is juicy, rather than wet, pour in the last of the stock. Stir as it simmers until the rice is tender with a bite at the centre. Cover and leave for 5 minutes, then mix in the last of the parsley. Serve the moist risotto with or without Parmesan.

Puddings

LYCHEES, MELON AND STEM
GINGER FRUIT SALAD

BLACK SWAN PAVLOVA

RHUBARB SYLLABUB TRIFLE

GOOSEBERRY AND ELDERFLOWER
ALMOND CRUMBLE

CHRISTIAN'S BELGIAN APPLE TART

VENETIAN RICE PUDDING WITH
MADAGASCAN BLACK CHOCOLATE

PINEAPPLE *TARTE TATIN*
WITH SWEET CHILLI

MALVA PUDDING

PEAR AND GINGER CHEESECAKE

CHOCOLATE RASPBERRY
SPONGE SANDWICH

Who'd have thought to put this disparate mix of ingredients together? Not me, but I was intrigued enough to adapt the recipe from a giant tin of lychees bought in an Oriental shop in Penzance, of all places. It turned out to be a triumph of texture and flavour. The leftover juices make a mean cocktail. You will not need cream, although a few chopped mint leaves look very pretty and smell fresh and vibrant.

LYCHEES, MELON AND STEM GINGER FRUIT SALAD SERVES 6–8

PREP: 20 MINUTES, PLUS
60 MINUTES TO CHILL

- *4 x 400g tins of lychees in light syrup*
- *2 ripe Galia melons*
- *8 globes stem ginger in syrup*
- *8 tablespoons stem ginger syrup*
- *a few mint leaves, optional*

Drain the lychees, reserving the liquid — keep it in a jar in the fridge. Tear them in half into a serving bowl, preferably a glass one. Halve the melon, remove the seeds and use a melon baller or cut it into kebab-size squares. Finely slice the ginger — I like thin large pieces but chop it smaller if you prefer. Add the melon, sliced ginger and ginger syrup to the lychees. Toss thoroughly and chill for at least an hour and up to 24. Toss again — it will be much juicier — taste the juice and add a little of the reserved lychee syrup if you think it is necessary. Serve the salad chilled, with or without chopped mint.

Pavlova is so popular in Australia that not everyone realizes it comes from New Zealand and, to be authentic, should include kiwi fruit. You can tell an Oz Pav because it's likely to feature passion fruit. My Pavlova is inspired by the movie *Black Swan* and the drama of a black fruit topping is stupendous. I like the sour-sweet tang of passion fruit, its black and yellow seeds with the sweet meringue and cream, and it unifies the black fruit like a layer of lace in a ballerina's tutu (the original inspiration for Pavlova). If some of the fruits are not available, no worries, just up the quantities of the others. Red currants, by the way, if black currants are not available, will stand out like jewels among the black fruit.

BLACK SWAN PAVLOVA SERVES 6–8

PREP: 15 MINUTES
COOK: 90 MINUTES, PLUS
2–4 HOURS COOLING

- *1 lemon*
- *4 egg whites at room temperature*
- *½ teaspoon cream of tartar*
- *100g white icing sugar*
- *300ml whipping cream*
- *100g seedless black grapes*
- *150g dark British cherries*
- *150g blackberries*
- *100g blueberries*
- *100g black or red currants*
- *4 passion fruit*

Heat the oven to 150°C/gas mark 1. Halve the lemon, and smear it around the spotlessly clean bowl of a mixer fitted with a whisk attachment. Add the egg whites. Start the machine slowly, increasing the speed as the whites froth. Add the cream of tartar, continuing at top speed until you have firm peaks. With the machine still running, add the icing sugar, a tablespoon at a time, until the mixture is glossy and stiff.

Pencil a 24cm circle on parchment paper, then dampen it with wet hands. Use a couple of dabs of meringue to 'glue' the paper to a baking sheet, then spread the meringue in the circle, making the sides slightly higher than the centre. Bake for 30 minutes, reduce to 100°C/gas mark ½ and cook for an hour until crisp and cracked on the outside, half cooked and soft inside. If the meringue starts to brown, turn off the oven and leave it to finish cooking as the oven cools. You are aiming for a snowy white Pavlova.

Leave to cool in the closed oven. Carefully peel the parchment paper off the meringue and transfer to a serving plate. Whip the cream and spoon it into the middle; the meringue may split or crack but that is part of its charm. Halve the grapes, stone the cherries and mix with the blackberries, blueberries and black currants. Tumble the fruit into the middle of the Pavlova and scrape the passion fruit seeds and juice over the top. Stand back for oohs and aahs.

for the rhubarb:
- *800g forced or young rhubarb*
- *100g caster sugar*
- *3 navel oranges*

for the trifle:
- *6 slices of Madeira or sponge cake*
- *100ml sweet sherry*

for the vanilla custard:
- *600ml milk*
- *½ split vanilla pod*
- *4 large egg yolks*
- *1 egg*
- *75g caster sugar (or 500g tub luxury thick and creamy custard)*

for the syllabub:
- *1 large lemon*
- *100ml sherry*
- *2 tablespoons brandy or whisky*
- *50g caster sugar*
- *300ml double cream*

to decorate:
- *3 tablespoons Seville orange marmalade*
- *2 tablespoons water*

Rhubarb isn't the obvious choice for a trifle but when it's poached in fresh orange juice and piled over sherry-soaked Madeira cake with homemade custard and boozy lemon syllabub it's worth all the effort. Instead of the usual sprinkles the decoration is jewel-like blobs of golden marmalade. Usefully, it can be made a couple of days ahead.

RHUBARB SYLLABUB TRIFLE SERVES 8

Begin with the syllabub. Mix the lemon juice, sherry and brandy in a bowl and stir in the caster sugar until it has dissolved. Add the cream gradually, whisking as you pour, continuing for at least 5 minutes until the mixture holds soft peaks. Leave in a cold place, not the fridge, until required.

Cut the rhubarb into 1cm-thick slices. Place in a medium pan with 75g of the sugar and 150ml of juice from the oranges. Cook gently over a medium-low heat, swirling the pan a few times as the sugar melts, for about 8 minutes until the rhubarb is almost tender. Use a slotted spoon to scoop it into a bowl to cool. Increase the heat and simmer briskly for 8 to 10 minutes until the juice is syrupy and reduced to about 5 tablespoons. Pour it over the rhubarb, stirring to mix. As it cools it will thicken.

Cut the cake to fit the base and go a little way up the sides of a glass bowl. Pour over the sherry to saturate. Spoon the rhubarb over the top. Allow the liquids to soak into the cake.

To make the custard, scald the milk with the split vanilla pod in the clean pan, giving it a few prods with a wooden spoon to disperse the seeds. Cover and leave to infuse for at least 20 minutes. Beat the egg yolks with the whole egg and the sugar in a mixing bowl. Strain the vanilla-flavoured milk over the egg and stir to mix before pouring it back into the pan. Cook very gently over a low heat, beating with a wooden spoon regularly to disperse hot spots, continuing until very thick with a slight wobble to the texture; allow at least 20 minutes for this. Let it cool slightly, then spoon over the rhubarb. Leave it to cool completely.

To finish the trifle, spoon and smooth, swirl or pipe the syllabub over the custard. To decorate, first heat the marmalade and water together, stirring as the marmalade melts. Scoop out the peel. Cook briefly until syrupy. Leave to cool and set. Place small blobs of the jelly around the edge of the trifle.

This crumble is a deviation from the usual mixture of flour, butter and sugar, replacing some of the flour with ground almonds. It's a combination that works particularly well with gooseberries. Their tart flavour is mellowed by the flowery tang of elderflower cordial and lime juice. Serve it hot, warm or cold. Good with clotted or Jersey cream.

GOOSEBERRY AND ELDERFLOWER ALMOND CRUMBLE SERVES 4–6

PREP: 20 MINUTES
COOK: 35 MINUTES

- *750g green gooseberries*
- *25g hard butter*
- *2 tablespoons caster sugar*
- *3 tablespoons elderflower cordial*
- *a squeeze of lime juice*

for the crumble:
- *100g caster sugar*
- *100g plain flour*
- *100g ground almonds*
- *a pinch of salt*
- *150g hard butter*

Heat the oven to 200°C/gas mark 6. Top and tail the gooseberries. Rinse and shake them dry, then tip them into a 1.5-litre gratin dish. Use a small sharp knife to shave the 25g of butter over the top. Sprinkle the caster sugar over the fruit and splash with the cordial. Add a squeeze of lime. Place in the oven as it comes up to temperature, then cook for 10 minutes while you make the crumble.

Mix the sugar, flour, almonds and salt in a bowl and cut the 150g of butter over the top. Quickly rub the butter into the dry ingredients, lifting and dropping it back as you go, continuing until the mixture is evenly crumbed. Spoon the crumble over the softening gooseberries, letting it trickle down between the fruit.

Return to the hot oven and cook until golden, checking after 20 minutes in case the crumble is colouring too quickly. If it is, lay a sheet of baking parchment over the top. Allow it to rest for at least 10 minutes before serving so the juices settle and the crumb won't burn your lips.

A dear friend of mine who used to run a restaurant in Chiswick was famous for this tart (and his cheese soufflés). At Christian's it was on the menu as Belgian apple tart, probably because the *chef-patron* was half Belgian. It's basically French apple tart with a custard background but the custard hardly gets a look-in because the tart is crammed with two circles of sliced apple. Christian always made his with Cox's Orange Pippins but any large eating apple would be suitable. I make it with imported Golden Delicious when Cox's aren't available.

It's an occasion for all-butter pastry made with egg and rolled quite thin so the tart is light and elegant. I make it in a tart tin with a removable base so it can be shown off in all its splendour. It is best eaten warm, although cold is better than hot when it will be a bit fragile. Very yum.

CHRISTIAN'S BELGIAN APPLE TART SERVES 6–8

PREP: 45 MINUTES
COOK: 45 MINUTES

• *You will need:* a 26cm tart tin with a removable base

for the pastry:
• *200g plain flour, plus extra for rolling and dusting*

• *a pinch of salt*

• *100g unsalted butter, plus an extra knob*

• *1 egg*

• *1 tablespoon water*

for the filling:
• *300ml thick cream*

• *4 large egg yolks*

• *4 tablespoons caster sugar, plus extra for sprinkling*

• *3–4 large Cox's Orange Pippins or Golden Delicious*

To make the pastry, sift the flour into a bowl with the salt. Cut the butter over the top and use your fingertips to rub it into the flour until it resembles breadcrumbs. Whisk the egg with the water and stir it into the mixture, continuing as it comes together. Knead lightly and briefly while you form it into a ball. Pop it into a plastic bag and chill for 30 minutes.

Heat the oven to 190°C/gas mark 5. Rub the knob of butter all over the inside of the tart tin. Add a tablespoon of flour, letting it dust the butter, and shake out the excess. Roll the pastry to fit the tin. Loosely cover it with foil and fill with baking beans. Bake for 10 minutes. Remove the foil and bake for a further 5 minutes.

Beat together the cream, egg yolks and 2 tablespoons of the sugar. Peel, quarter and core the apples. Make 5 or 6 thin slices, lengthways, from each quarter. Arrange them on the tart base, in two overlapping circles, starting on the outside, using the last few slices to fill gaps in and around the middle. Ladle the custard over the top. Dust with the remaining 2 tablespoons of sugar. Place on a baking sheet and bake for 45 minutes until the apple is tender, the custard just set and the top golden. Sprinkle with a little caster sugar then rest for 5 minutes. Stand it on a tin to remove the collar. Slide the tart off the metal base onto a plate and admire.

This rice pudding is actually a sweet risotto made with milk and cream, flavoured with vanilla and nutmeg, orange and lemon, and thick with plump sultanas soaked in Marsala. It's not the most beautiful rice pudding in appearance, but a generous grating from a block of rich, dark chocolate, looks and tastes stupendous. I'd particularly recommend Madagascan Black from www.williescacao.com (for stockists).

VENETIAN RICE PUDDING WITH MADAGASCAN BLACK CHOCOLATE SERVES 6

PREP: 15 MINUTES
COOK: 45 MINUTES

• 125g golden sultanas

• 150ml Marsala

• 1 vanilla pod

• 1 medium navel orange

• 1 lemon

• a pinch of salt

• 50g caster sugar

• 700ml milk

• 300ml double cream

• 150ml arborio rice

• 180g bar of Willie's Madagascan Black (100% pure cacao) chocolate

Place the sultanas and Marsala in a pan that can hold all of the ingredients. Simmer together for a few minutes over a very low heat until the sultanas are swollen with booze. Tip them into a bowl.

Split the vanilla pod and place it in the pan with the zest and juice from the orange and lemon, a pinch of salt, the sugar, milk and cream. Bring slowly to a simmer, stirring until the sugar has melted, then add the rice, the sultanas and any juice.

Cook, stirring every few minutes, for about 30 minutes, until it is thick, creamy, and the rice is soft. Serve risotto-style with a fork, passing the chocolate for people to grate over the top.

I once stayed at a hotel in Mauritius where they served cocktails with little kebabs of lightly salted pineapple and scraps of chilli. It seemed odd at first but it's a combination I grew to like. For this version of the famous caramelized upside-down tart, I've used salted butter and served it with a splash of sweet chilli sauce. It's fantastic. As always with *tarte Tatin*, gauging how far to go with caramelizing the sugar and butter is tricky. I like it quite dark, so the juices taste almost burned, but some people prefer a lighter caramel flavour. A tip: pour most of the juices off before the tart is inverted. I discovered the hard way why this is a good idea. Serve hot with lemony crème fraîche.

PINEAPPLE *TARTE TATIN* WITH SWEET CHILLI SERVES 6

PREP: 30 MINUTES
COOK: 30 MINUTES

• *You will need:* a 20cm tarte Tatin tin, or a similarly shaped (sloping sides, heavy-bottomed) 20cm ovenproof frying pan

for the filling:
• *1 ripe pineapple*
• *150g light brown sugar*
• *75g salted butter*

for the pastry:
• *200g plain flour, plus extra for dusting*
• *a pinch of salt*
• *100g salted butter*
• *1 egg*
• *1 tablespoon water*

to serve:
• *crème fraîche*
• *Thai sweet chilli sauce*

First make the pastry. Sift the flour into a bowl with the salt. Cut the butter over the top and use your fingertips to rub it into the flour until it resembles breadcrumbs. Whisk the egg with the water and stir into the mixture, continuing as it comes together. Knead lightly and briefly while you form it into a ball. Pop it into a plastic bag and chill for 30 minutes.

Peel the pineapple and slice it 2cm thick, then slice it into three pieces around the hard central core. Melt the sugar and butter together in the frying pan, stirring as it begins to colour, continuing until the syrup turns a deep gold, like toffee. Don't worry about the changes it goes through, sometimes Vesuvial, sometimes gravelly: they really don't matter. Remove from the heat and leave to cool slightly. Carefully arrange the pieces of pineapple into the hot caramel, fitting them together like a jigsaw, cutting some pieces to fill any gaps.

Heat the oven to 200°C/gas mark 6. On a floured surface, roll the pastry to fit the pan. Carefully lay it over the top and trim off the excess. Now tuck the pastry down inside the rim; it will naturally form a wavy pattern because it will be too large due to the sloping sides of the pan. Bake for 30 minutes or until the pastry is golden brown and cooked through.

Let it rest for 5 minutes — some of the juices will soak back into the pineapple — then carefully pour off excess juice into a jug. Lay a large plate over the top of the tart and invert quickly, watching out for the hot juices as you turn. Drizzle with the sweet chilli sauce and serve with crème fraîche. Use this recipe as a template for the real McCoy, using 8 to 12 Cox's apples, peeled, cored and quartered.

There are times when a good old-fashioned comfort pudding is the order of the day. I came across this one after my first *braai* (South African barbecue) and fell in love with its firm, almost springy texture, which glistens like a baked sponge and is creamily caramelized with a vanilla back-taste. It's rich and luscious like sticky toffee pudding without the dates and very moreish.

The type of sugar it's made with radically alters the look and flavour of the pudding. I used white for the sponge and brown for the sauce, which soaks into the pudding, giving a pleasant mottled effect and a rich flavour. Using white for both results in a pale pudding, while brown makes it dark and mysterious. Palm sugar, if you can get the real thing, gives fabulous results and so does richly flavoured Tate & Lyle's Golden Syrup Sugar. Serve the pudding hot or cold, on its own, with cream, custard or both.

MALVA PUDDING SERVES 6–8

PREP: 20 MINUTES
COOK: 50 MINUTES

- *You will need:* a 2-litre (5cm deep) gratin-style ceramic or glass dish
- *250g self-raising flour*
- *150g sugar*
- *1 teaspoon bicarbonate of soda*
- *1 egg*
- *250ml milk*
- *25g butter*
- *1 tablespoon golden syrup*
- *½ teaspoon vanilla extract*

for the sauce:
- *250ml whipping cream*
- *125g butter*
- *125g molasses sugar*
- *125ml water*

Heat the oven to 170°C/gas mark 3. Sift the flour into a bowl (preferably of a blender) and mix in the sugar and bicarbonate of soda. Add the egg and milk. Melt the butter and golden syrup together, stir in the vanilla extract and add to the other ingredients. Blend smooth to make a thick batter. Pour it into the gratin-style dish. Rest a sheet of foil over the top to cover loosely. Bake on the top shelf of the oven for 40 to 50 minutes until firm to a flat hand and golden at the edges.

While the pudding bakes, heat the sauce ingredients, stirring until the sugar melts. This is done slowly in a bowl over a pan of boiling water from a kettle, or by cheating with a small pan over direct heat! Make holes all over the pudding with a kebab stick or similar and pour over the hot sauce; the holes encourage the sauce to soak in. Serve hot, warm or cold, with custard or vanilla ice cream.

The cream for this cheesecake is laced with little scraps of stem ginger. They echo the mildly gingery flavour of a thin biscuit base made with crumbly Cornish Fairings or other ginger and honey biscuits. The topping is fluffy and very pale creamy yellow and it takes a moment to recognize it as puréed pear. By cheesecake standards, this one is slim in depth but fat with flavour. It is made in a tart tin with a removable base so it can be served in all its splendour on a cake stand.

PEAR AND GINGER CHEESECAKE SERVES 6–8

PREP: 30 MINUTES, PLUS MINIMUM 3 HOURS CHILLING
COOK: 15 MINUTES

• *You will need:* a 22cm loose-bottomed flan tin

• *200g ginger and honey Cornish Fairings or similar biscuits*

• *75g butter*

• *400g tin pears in fruit juice*

• *a squeeze of lemon*

• *1 sheet of gelatine*

• *25g soft butter*

• *25g sugar*

• *150g thick cream*

• *4 globes stem ginger*

• *300g full-fat cream cheese or mascarpone*

Break the biscuits into the bowl of a food processor and blitz to crumbs. Melt the butter, add to the crumbs, pulsing or stirring to make a crumbly paste. Tip it into the flan tin. Spread the biscuit mixture evenly with a spatula, then use the base of a tumbler to compact it. Cover with clingfilm and pop it into the freezer or chill in the fridge for at least an hour.

Blitz the drained pears, the lemon juice and a tablespoon of the fruit juice from the tin into a smooth purée. Soften the gelatine in sufficient water to cover. Warm the pear purée in a small pan – on no account let it simmer or boil – then, off the heat, stir in the floppy gelatine until it has dissolved. Pour the mixture into a bowl and chill.

Cream the soft butter with the sugar until it is light and fluffy. Whisk the cream until it holds firm peaks in a separate bowl. Chop the ginger into small scraps the size of a shirt button. Stir the cream cheese or mascarpone and ginger into the sugary butter then fold in the cream. Spread the stiff cheese mixture over the chilled base then top with a smooth layer of chilled pear purée. Cover with a tight stretch of clingfilm, avoiding it touching the pears, and chill for at least 2 hours. Remove the clingfilm, stand the cheesecake on a tin and carefully ease off the collar. Finely slice the remaining globe of ginger into skinny batons and use to decorate the cake.

This is the best way of making a Victoria sponge, weighing the eggs and using the same weight of flour, sugar and butter with a teaspoonful of baking powder for good measure. It's a simple way of remembering the quantities and produces a reliably good sponge sandwich. The classic filling is jam, with cream for luxury, the top dusted with icing sugar. This chocolate version is the cake my mother made for high days and holidays, and always on my birthday. She filled it with whipped cream and big chunks of strawberry, and decorated the top with crumbled Cadbury's Flake. I like the softer squishy effect of raspberries too, but both soft fruits are delicious, and so are cherries (stoned).

CHOCOLATE RASPBERRY SPONGE SANDWICH SERVES 6

PREP: 25 MINUTES
COOK: 25 MINUTES

- *You will need:* 2 x 18cm loose-base sponge tins
- *3 medium eggs*
- *soft butter (approx. 180g), plus an extra knob*
- *caster sugar (approx. 180g)*
- *self-raising flour (approx. 180g)*
- *3 level tablespoons cocoa*
- *1 teaspoon baking powder*
- *300ml whipping cream*
- *icing sugar*
- *400g raspberries or small British strawberries*

Heat the oven to 180°C/gas mark 4. Weigh the eggs in their shells. Whatever the weight, measure the same of butter and sugar. Make up the flour in the same way, incorporating the cocoa within its weight. Add the baking powder. Using an electric whisk or wooden spoon, cream the butter and sugar until they are light and fluffy. Add the eggs, one at a time with a spoonful of the flour mix. Using a large metal spoon, gently but quickly stir the remaining flour into the mixture until it is smooth, thick and creamy.

Lightly butter the sponge tins. Place a disc of baking parchment in the base (the butter helps it stick) and divide the mixture between the tins, gently smoothing the top. Place them side by side on the middle shelf in the hot oven and cook for about 20 minutes or until the cakes feel firm and bouncy to the flat of your hand.

Remove them from the oven, leave for 5 minutes, then turn onto a wire cake rack to cool. Whip the cream until it forms soft peaks with a tablespoon of icing sugar. Place one cake on a plate or cake stand. Lay dollops of cream on top, then spread them smoothly. Add half of the hulled raspberries. Gently top with the second sponge. Spread the top with more cream and arrange the rest of the raspberries randomly or neatly in circles. Dust with icing sugar and admire your work.

COOK'S NOTES

INDEX

Page references for photographs are in **bold**

red peppers: gazpacho Andaluz 78, **79**
rhubarb syllabub trifle 200
ribs: sticky pork ribs with potatoes 55
rice:
    Costas' mussels **182**, 183
    Louisiana jambalaya 184, **185**
    Moroccan lemon and chicken pilaff **186**, 187
    paella bianco 188
    risi e bisi 189
    risotto with sausage, beans and red wine 192, **193**
    saffron onion rice with chicken and peas **190**, 191
    summer kedgeree with lime 180, **181**
    Venetian rice pudding with Madagascan black
        chocolate 204, **205**
risi e bisi 189
risotto:
    red orzo risotto with goat's cheese **146**, 147
    risotto with sausage, beans and red wine 192, **193**
    Venetian rice pudding with Madagascan black
        chocolate 204, **205**
rocket and feta pasta with fresh tomato sauce 144, **145**
rouille: Cornish fish stew with *rouille* **100**, 101

S
saffron:
    saffron chicken with apricots and cardamom 132,
        133
    saffron onion rice with chicken and peas **190**, 191
salami and mushroom hash 24, **25**
salmon:
    salmon *confit*, brown shrimp and samphire
        noodles **166**, 167
    salmon and tomato curry **130**, 131
    warm Puy lentils with poached salmon and
        leeks **42**, 43
samphire:
    beluga lentils, beetroot, samphire and
        anchovy **30**, 31
    salmon *confit*, brown shrimp and samphire
        noodles **166**, 167
sauerkraut: poached frankfurters with caraway
    sauerkraut 94
sausages:
    braised chicken, Toulouse sausages and white beans
        60, **61**
    poached frankfurters with caraway sauerkraut 94
    poached sausages, celery and potatoes 21
    risotto with sausage, beans and red wine 192, **193**
    sausage and lentil stew 115, **115**
    see also chorizo; salami

scallops: Cornish fish stew with *rouille* **100**, 101
sea bass: baked Provençal sea bass with potatoes 54
seafood:
    cod and prawn tom yam 81
    Cornish fish stew with *rouille* **100**, 101
    Costas' mussels **182**, 183
    fideua con allioli 158, **159**
    ginger prawns with Vietnamese noodle salad 37
    hot and sour prawn noodles 168
    Louisiana jambalaya 184, **185**
    moules à la Provençale 86, **87**
    Mumbai prawn pasta 128, **129**
    pad Thai 164
    prawn, fennel, new potatoes and peas 82, **83**
    salmon *confit*, brown shrimp and samphire
        noodles **166**, 167
    seafood *laksa* 162, **163**
    Singapore noodles 165
    spaghetti *alle vongole bianco* 152, **153**
    squid, chorizo and chickpea *cocido* 102, **103**
sesame seeds: Szechuan chicken salad with peanut
    and sesame 44, **45**
shrimps:
    salmon *confit*, brown shrimp and samphire
        noodles **166**, 167
    Singapore noodles 165
Singapore noodles 165
skirt steak: *bavette*, artichoke and haricot salad 46, **47**
sliders: pulled belly pork sliders, with apple
    sauce 64, **65**
slipper aubergine, tomato and goat's cheese 50, **51**
smoked mackerel croquettes with beetroot purée 18, 19
sole: flat peas and sole, lime and ginger stir-fry 20
spaghetti:
    black pasta with garlic olive oil and chilli 148, **149**
    fresh spaghetti with leeks, Parma ham and
        hazelnuts 157
    spaghetti *alle vongole bianco* 152, **153**
spezzatino: veal *spezzatino* 118, **119**
spinach:
    ham and spinach strata with green sauce 62, 63
    spinach tagliatelle with asparagus, goat's cheese and
        San Daniele **150**, 151
    Sri Lankan chicken curry with sweet potato and
        spinach 136, **137**
spring chicken with lemon potatoes 58, 59
spring chicken stew with carrots and peas **104**, 105
squash: Moroccan chicken and butternut squash
    tagine 108

ACKNOWLEDGEMENTS

So many people work behind the scenes to make a book special. For this one, I'd particularly like to thank Lindsey Evans, cookery publisher at Penguin, for asking me to write it and for my agent Andrew Gordon and his assistant Marigold Atkey at David Higham for clinching the deal. On a more practical level, I'd like to thank Chris Terry (and his assistant, Danny Treacy) for producing such appetizing photos, and a team of home economists led by Lisa Harrison and Anna Burges-Lumsden, not forgetting prop stylist Emma Lahaye, who worked tirelessly at Factory Studios on some of the hottest days of the year. Together they interpreted my food brilliantly. Thank you also to Sarah Fraser for her elegant book design, to Beatrix McIntyre for overseeing the final stages of the manuscript and for everyone else at Penguin for their support. Red, my constant companion, would like to thank her friends at Factory, particularly the black Lab on the top floor, who made her so welcome.

ABOUT THE AUTHOR

Lindsey Bareham is one of the UK's most talented cookery writers. Her daily after-work recipe column for the *Evening Standard* ran for eight years and she currently writes the much-loved 'Dinner Tonight' column for *The Times*. The author of thirteen cookery books, including *In Praise of the Potato*, *A Celebration of Soup*, *The Fish Store* and *The Trifle Bowl and Other Tales*, Lindsey also co-wrote *The Prawn Cocktail Years* with Simon Hopkinson, and helped him write *Roast Chicken and Other Stories*, voted the Most Useful Cookery Book Ever by chefs and food writers.